# THE AI SIDE HUSTLE REVOLUTION

YOUR GUIDE TO BUILDING
AI-POWERED BUSINESSES

edmond worth
profitbootcamp.ai

Copyright © 2024 Edmond Worth
All rights reserved.

No part of this publication may be reproduced, distributed, or transmitted in any form or by any means, including photocopying, recording, or other electronic or mechanical methods, without the prior written permission of the publisher, except in the case of brief quotations embodied in critical reviews and certain other noncommercial uses permitted by copyright law.

First Edition
Published by profitbootcamp.ai

**CONTENTS**

# Introduction 1

# A Note from the Author 3

# 1 The AI Side Hustle Revolution 5

Why 2025 is the AI Gold Rush . . . . . . . . . . . . . . . . . . . . . . 6
The Evolution of AI Tools . . . . . . . . . . . . . . . . . . . . . . . . 6
Why 2025 is Different . . . . . . . . . . . . . . . . . . . . . . . . . . 6
The Current Opportunity Landscape . . . . . . . . . . . . . . . . . . . 7
The Perfect Timing . . . . . . . . . . . . . . . . . . . . . . . . . . . . 7
The AI Leverage Advantage . . . . . . . . . . . . . . . . . . . . . . . 8
Types of AI Side Hustles . . . . . . . . . . . . . . . . . . . . . . . . . 9
Getting Started . . . . . . . . . . . . . . . . . . . . . . . . . . . . . . 10
Building Blocks of Success . . . . . . . . . . . . . . . . . . . . . . . . 12
Common Myths and Realities . . . . . . . . . . . . . . . . . . . . . . 14
Your Action Plan . . . . . . . . . . . . . . . . . . . . . . . . . . . . . 15
Chapter Summary . . . . . . . . . . . . . . . . . . . . . . . . . . . . 17

# 2 Essential AI Tools & Setup 21

Understanding AI Platforms . . . . . . . . . . . . . . . . . . . . . . . 21
Automation Tools . . . . . . . . . . . . . . . . . . . . . . . . . . . . . 23
Business Infrastructure . . . . . . . . . . . . . . . . . . . . . . . . . . 24
Setting Up Your Tech Stack . . . . . . . . . . . . . . . . . . . . . . . 25
Building Your Workflows . . . . . . . . . . . . . . . . . . . . . . . . . 26
Quality Control Systems . . . . . . . . . . . . . . . . . . . . . . . . . 27
Cost & Performance Management . . . . . . . . . . . . . . . . . . . . 28
Your Implementation Path . . . . . . . . . . . . . . . . . . . . . . . . 30
Chapter Summary . . . . . . . . . . . . . . . . . . . . . . . . . . . . 30

# 3 Setting Up Your Technical Foundation — 33

- Your AI Workspace — 33
- Organization & Storage — 34
- Testing & Iteration — 35
- Protection & Costs — 36
- Chapter Summary — 37

# 4 Five Proven AI Business Models — 39

- AI Service Arbitrage — 40
- Custom GPT Development — 41
- AI-Powered Content Systems — 42
- Prompt Engineering Services — 43
- AI Business Consultation — 44
- Model Selection Framework — 46
- Combining Business Models — 47
- Chapter Summary — 49

# 5 AI Service Arbitrage — 51

- Choosing Your Service — 52
- Market Research and Validation — 54
- Understanding Your Pricing — 55
- Service Validation and Minimum Viable Service — 58
- Service Setup Guide — 59
- Getting Your First Client — 65
- Delivery System — 69
- Chapter Summary — 75

# 6 Custom GPT Development — 79

- Understanding the Market — 81
- Development Process — 85
- Store Listing & Monetization — 90
- Marketing Your GPT — 93
- User Support Systems — 95
- Growth & Scaling — 98
- Chapter Summary — 100

# 7 AI-Powered Content Systems — 103

- Understanding Content Systems — 103
- Content System Possibilities — 104
- Your First Steps — 108
- Building Your Content Engine — 109

|     |                                       |     |
| --- | ------------------------------------- | --- |
|     | Automation Fundamentals (500 words)   | 111 |
|     | Distribution & Monetization           | 131 |
|     | Growth & Optimization                 | 133 |
|     | Chapter Summary                       | 134 |

## 8 Prompt Engineering Services — 137

Understanding the Market — 137
Building Your Service Foundation — 139
Service Packages — 140
Implementation Examples — 142
Delivery Systems — 143
Growth & Scaling — 144
Chapter Summary — 145

## 9 AI Business Consultation — 149

Understanding the Market — 150
Your Consultation Foundation — 151
Service Packages — 153
Real-World Examples — 154
Delivery Process — 156
Growth & Scaling — 157
Chapter Summary — 159

## 10 Advanced AI Strategies — 163

Opening Hook — 163
AI Product Development — 164
Custom Model Development — 165
Advanced Automation Systems — 167
Building AI-Powered Apps — 169
Premium Service Opportunities — 170
Future-Proofing Strategies — 172
Chapter Summary — 173

## 11 Your AI Journey: Next Steps — 177

Essential Skills to Develop — 177
Building Your Support System — 178
Common Challenges and Solutions — 179
Final Thoughts — 180

# Introduction

The AI revolution has created unprecedented opportunities for side hustles and small businesses. But most books about AI entrepreneurship either get lost in technical details or make unrealistic promises about overnight success. This book is different.

This is a practical guide for building real AI-powered side businesses that you can run alongside your day job. You won't find complex machine learning theory or get-rich-quick schemes here. Instead, you'll learn proven business models, step-by-step implementation guides, and practical strategies that work in the real world.

### What This Book Will Do

- Show you five proven AI business models you can start with minimal technical expertise
- Provide detailed implementation guides for each business model
- Walk you through the tools, systems, and processes you need
- Show you how to grow while maintaining work-life balance
- Help you avoid common pitfalls and mistakes

### What This Book Won't Do

- Teach you to code or build AI models from scratch
- Promise unrealistic income or results
- Require you to quit your day job
- Overwhelm you with technical jargon
- Suggest high-risk or unethical approaches

## How to Use This Book

Start with Chapter 1 to understand the AI side hustle landscape. Then read Chapter 2-3 to set up your technical foundation. From there, choose one of the five business models (Chapters 5-9) that interests you most and follow its implementation guide. Use Chapters 10-11 when you're ready to grow beyond the basics.

Remember, success in AI entrepreneurship isn't about having the most advanced technology - it's about solving real problems for real people. Let's begin your journey into practical AI entrepreneurship.

## A Note from the Author

This book isn't about how I built a billion-dollar AI empire or achieved overnight success. Instead, it's a practical guide that combines my software development background with extensive research into how AI is transforming the side hustle landscape.

I wrote this book because I saw an opportunity: AI tools are making it possible for regular people to build profitable side businesses, but most guides are either too technical or too vague to be useful.

My goal was to create something different - a clear, step-by-step guide that helps you:

- Understand what's actually possible
- Choose an approach that fits your life
- Build something real with today's tools
- Avoid common pitfalls
- Get to first revenue without quitting your day job

Think of this as the guide I wish I had when I started exploring AI business opportunities. It won't make you a billionaire, but it will show you how to build something real in your spare time.

# A NOTE FROM THE AUTHOR

CHAPTER 1

# The AI Side Hustle Revolution

We're living through one of the most significant technological shifts in human history. Artificial Intelligence has moved from science fiction to practical reality, transforming how we work, create, and build businesses. But unlike previous technological revolutions that required massive investments or specialized degrees, the AI revolution is uniquely accessible to side hustlers and entrepreneurs.

This accessibility isn't just about the technology itself – it's about the unprecedented combination of powerful tools, low barriers to entry, and the ability to automate complex tasks. For the first time, individuals can leverage enterprise-grade AI capabilities from their laptops, building automated systems that work while they sleep.

The timing is particularly significant. We've moved past the initial hype cycle of AI, where speculation and uncertainty dominated the conversation. Now, in 2025, we're entering a phase where the real, practical applications of AI are becoming clear. The tools have matured, the use cases have been validated, and businesses of all sizes are actively seeking AI solutions.

This creates a unique opportunity for side hustlers – the ability to build sustainable, automated income streams without quitting your day job. But to seize this opportunity, you need to understand both the possibilities and the principles that make AI side hustles work. This book will show you how to navigate this landscape, avoid common pitfalls, and build systems that can grow while you maintain your primary career.

## Why 2025 is the AI Gold Rush

The AI landscape of 2025 is radically different from the chaotic gold rush of 2023-2024. While early adopters scrambled to capitalize on new AI tools, often with mixed results, we're now entering what industry experts call "The Age of AI Implementation." This maturation presents unprecedented opportunities for side hustlers who can leverage proven strategies and established tools.

## The Evolution of AI Tools

When ChatGPT burst onto the scene in late 2022, it sparked a frenzy of speculation and experimentation. Few could have predicted how dramatically the landscape would change in just a few years. Today's AI platforms have evolved from exciting but unreliable novelties into robust, dependable business tools. ChatGPT, Claude, and their contemporaries now offer the kind of stability and consistency that businesses can truly rely on.

Perhaps most significantly, the cost of AI operations has finally stabilized. The early days of unpredictable pricing and expensive API calls are behind us. What once required costly GPT-4 credits can now be accomplished with more affordable, specialized models. This price stability has opened the door for sustainable, profitable business models that simply weren't possible during the initial boom.

The integration ecosystem has also matured beautifully. Gone are the days when leveraging AI required deep technical expertise or coding skills. Today's no-code tools and integration platforms have democratized AI implementation, making it accessible to anyone with a clear vision and strong business sense.

## Why 2025 is Different

The key difference between now and the early AI boom comes down to market maturity. We're no longer in uncharted territory, guessing at what might work. The market has validated specific business models, providing clear pathways to success for newcomers. Early adopters paid a heavy "pioneer tax," learning expensive lessons about what works and what doesn't. Today, you can benefit from these insights without paying that same price.

Perhaps most importantly, the market itself has evolved. Businesses no longer need convincing that AI solutions are worthwhile – they're actively seeking them out. The conversation has shifted from "Why should we use AI?" to "How can we implement AI effectively?" This shift creates a perfect opportunity for side hustlers who can deliver results.

### The Current Opportunity Landscape

The most promising opportunities in 2025 have crystallized around three main areas: implementation services, specialized AI products, and AI-powered traditional services. Implementation services – helping businesses integrate and optimize AI tools – have become particularly attractive. With the right systems and automation in place, these services can be delivered efficiently while maintaining high value for clients.

Specialized AI products have emerged as another sweet spot. Rather than competing with generic AI tools, successful entrepreneurs are creating niche solutions for specific industries. These specialized tools often generate reliable recurring revenue while requiring minimal ongoing maintenance once properly automated.

The third major opportunity lies in using AI to deliver traditional services more efficiently. This approach combines the best of both worlds: the established demand of traditional services with the competitive advantage and higher margins that AI enables.

### The Perfect Timing

While the market has matured, we're still early in the broader AI revolution. Think of it like the internet in the early 2000s – past the wild speculation of the late '90s, but still with vast untapped potential. The current landscape offers a rare combination of proven models to follow, established tools to leverage, and educated customers ready to buy.

This combination makes 2025 the ideal time to start an AI side hustle. The market is mature enough to be predictable, yet young enough to offer significant opportunities for newcomers. The gold rush mentality has faded, replaced by something more valuable: a stable, growing market with clear paths to profitability.

But to truly capitalize on this opportunity, you need to understand what makes AI side hustles fundamentally different from traditional businesses. This difference lies in what we call the automation advantage.

## The AI Leverage Advantage

The real power of AI side hustles isn't just in the technology itself – it's in the leverage it provides. While traditional side hustles often create a second job for themselves, AI entrepreneurs use technology to multiply their impact. This fundamental difference changes everything about how you can approach building additional income streams.

Think about a traditional freelance writer. They might spend hours crafting each article, trading their time directly for money. Now consider an AI-enhanced content service. The core work shifts from writing every word to orchestrating a powerful combination of AI capabilities and human expertise. You might use AI to generate initial drafts and handle research, enhance the content with your industry knowledge, and automate the delivery and distribution process. Instead of trading hours for dollars, you're creating systems that scale.

This approach is particularly attractive for people with full-time jobs. Your time investment becomes strategic – you focus on the aspects of the business where your expertise adds the most value, while using AI to handle everything else.

Well-designed AI systems can help you deliver higher quality results more reliably, handle increased workload without proportional time increases, and even expand into areas that would be impossible through pure human effort. This reliability and scalability is what allows you to build a reputation for exceptional delivery.

Rather than trying to automate everything, successful AI entrepreneurs focus on finding the right balance. They use AI to handle routine tasks while applying their judgment, creativity, and strategic thinking where it matters most. This might mean using AI for initial content but applying your expertise for strategic insights, or using automated systems for client onboarding while maintaining personal relationships for strategic discussions.

In the next section, we'll explore the specific types of AI side hustles that best leverage this advantage, showing you how different businesses strike this balance in practice.

## Types of AI Side Hustles

When it comes to building an AI-powered side hustle, there are three main approaches, each leveraging AI in different ways. Understanding these different models will help you choose the path that best fits your skills, time availability, and how you want to apply AI's capabilities.

The first approach is service-based. Here, you're using AI to enhance and scale traditional professional services. Think of a market research consultant who uses AI to analyze vast amounts of data, but applies their expertise to draw meaningful conclusions. Or a content strategist who uses AI to generate and optimize content, but provides the crucial strategic direction that AI cannot. The beauty of this approach is that you're entering markets that already understand and value these services. Your advantage comes from using AI to deliver better results while maintaining the human expertise clients trust.

The second approach is product-based. Instead of delivering services directly, you're creating tools, templates, or systems that help others leverage AI effectively. This might mean developing specialized GPTs that solve industry-specific problems, creating AI workflow templates, or building training systems that help others use AI tools more effectively. The advantage here is scalability

– once you've created the product, you can sell it multiple times with minimal additional effort. The key is finding specific problems where AI can provide consistent value when properly guided by your expertise.

The third approach is what we call the hybrid model, combining elements of both services and products. You might start with a service business, using AI to deliver exceptional results, then package your most effective processes into products. Or you might begin with an AI product but offer premium services where you personally help clients get better results. This flexibility allows you to build multiple revenue streams while leveraging both AI capabilities and your personal expertise in different ways.

Each of these approaches offers different ways to create leverage. Service-based businesses use AI to enhance human expertise and scale delivery. Product-based businesses leverage AI through systematic solutions that can be widely distributed. Hybrid models create leverage by combining both approaches strategically.

The key to choosing between these approaches isn't just about potential profitability – it's about how you want to apply AI's capabilities alongside your own expertise. Consider not just your technical skills, but how you prefer to work. Do you enjoy direct client interaction, where AI enhances your service delivery? Or would you rather create systems and products where AI operates within frameworks you design? Perhaps you'd prefer a mix of both?

Remember, you're not locked into your initial choice. Many successful AI entrepreneurs start with one approach and gradually expand into others as they learn more about both AI's capabilities and their own strengths. The important thing is to start with a model where you can effectively combine AI's power with your unique advantages.

## Getting Started

Starting an AI side hustle requires careful consideration of three key resources: time, skills, and tools. Understanding how to leverage these resources effectively will set you up for sustainable success without overwhelming your existing commitments.

Let's start with time – often the most precious resource for side hustlers. The beauty of AI-powered businesses is that they allow for strategic time investment. Rather than trading hours for dollars, you're investing time in building systems and expertise that create ongoing value. Think in terms of phases: an initial learning and setup phase where you'll need focused time to understand your tools and build your frameworks, followed by an optimization phase where you're refining your systems and expanding your impact.

Don't fall into the trap of thinking AI will eliminate the need for your time entirely. Instead, focus on using AI to make your time more valuable. If you can only spare five hours a week, that's fine – use AI to enhance those hours rather than trying to stretch them further. The goal is to build systems where AI handles routine tasks while you focus on high-impact activities that showcase your expertise.

When it comes to skills, you might be surprised by what you don't need. You don't need to be a programmer or an AI expert to build a successful AI side hustle. What you do need is the ability to think strategically about how AI can enhance your existing expertise. Success requires three core capabilities: First, strategic thinking to understand where AI can create the most leverage in your business. Second, solid business fundamentals that help you identify customer needs and create real value. Third, process design skills that enable you to build systems combining AI and human expertise effectively.

As for tools, the essential requirements are surprisingly modest. You'll need reliable access to AI platforms like ChatGPT or Claude, basic workflow tools, and standard business software. But more important than the tools themselves is understanding how to use them strategically. Start with the minimum viable setup and expand based on real needs – many successful AI entrepreneurs began with just a handful of basic tools and added more sophisticated options only as their business grew.

The key is to begin with clear intentions about how you'll use AI to create leverage. Are you using it to enhance your existing expertise? To scale your service delivery? To create products that solve specific problems? Your answer will guide your initial setup and help you focus your learning efforts where they'll create the most value.

## Building Blocks of Success

Every successful AI side hustle is built on a foundation of core systems and processes. Think of these as the building blocks that, when properly assembled, create a business that can run smoothly even while you maintain your day job.

The first essential building block is your leverage framework. This isn't just about using AI tools – it's about creating workflows that combine AI capabilities with your expertise in a meaningful way. Your framework should identify where AI can enhance your work, where it can handle tasks independently, and where your personal touch creates the most value. The goal is to create a system where every hour you invest has the maximum possible impact.

Customer acquisition forms another crucial building block. You need a reliable way to attract and engage potential clients or customers. This doesn't mean building complex marketing campaigns – often, the most effective approach is creating a simple, repeatable process for reaching your target market. The key is leveraging AI to handle the routine aspects of marketing and sales while maintaining authentic human connections where they matter most. Your outreach might be AI-enhanced, but your relationships should be genuinely yours.

Pricing strategy is another fundamental element that many overlook. In the AI-enhanced space, value-based pricing often works better than hourly rates or standard product pricing. This means structuring your offerings around the value they deliver rather than the time they take to produce. A well-designed pricing structure should reflect both the efficiency of your AI-enhanced systems and the unique value of your expertise. Remember, clients aren't paying for AI – they're paying for results.

Quality control becomes even more critical when working with AI. You need robust processes for ensuring that your AI-enhanced work maintains consistently high standards. This means developing clear quality benchmarks, implementing systematic review processes, and knowing exactly where human oversight adds the most value. The goal isn't to check everything manually – it's to create intelligent quality systems that flag potential issues while letting solid work flow through smoothly.

Risk management is the final key building block. This means having contingency plans for common scenarios: backup approaches for when AI tools don't perform as expected, alternative workflows for unusual requests, and clear boundaries for what your business will and won't do. Good risk management isn't about avoiding all risks – it's about being prepared to handle challenges while staying within your comfort zone.

These building blocks work together to create a resilient business structure. The goal isn't perfection from day one, but rather having a solid foundation that you can build upon as your side hustle grows.

> **ACTION ITEMS**
>
> - [ ] Calculate your realistic weekly time availability (considering work, family, and other commitments)
> - [ ] List your current professional expertise and strengths
> - [ ] Write down 3-5 areas where you think AI could amplify your existing skills
> - [ ] Research the current costs of basic AI tools (ChatGPT, Claude, etc.)
> - [ ] Identify which type of AI side hustle interests you most (service, product, or hybrid)
> - [ ] Write down your "unfair advantages" - unique combinations of skills or experience
> - [ ] List potential niches where your expertise meets market needs
> - [ ] Set a specific learning goal for the next 30 days
> - [ ] Block out specific weekly time slots for your side hustle development

## Common Myths and Realities

When it comes to AI side hustles, there are several persistent myths that can either discourage people from starting or lead them down the wrong path. Let's separate fact from fiction to give you a clearer picture of what's really possible.

The first myth is that you need to be a technical expert to succeed with AI. The reality is that most successful AI side hustles are built on business fundamentals rather than technical expertise. While you'll need to learn how to use specific tools, the more important skills are understanding customer needs, creating efficient processes, and delivering consistent value. The technical aspects can be learned incrementally as you grow.

Another common myth is that AI will do all the work for you. While AI tools are powerful, they're not magical. Success comes from thoughtfully combining AI capabilities with human insight and expertise. Think of AI as a powerful collaborator rather than a replacement. Your role isn't to disappear from the business – it's to focus your energy where your unique perspective and expertise create the most value.

Many people believe that the market is already saturated with AI businesses. The reality is that we're still in the early stages of AI adoption across many industries. What's more, the market isn't looking for generic AI services – it's looking for specialized solutions to specific problems. There's always room for businesses that combine AI capabilities with genuine expertise to deliver real value in focused niches.

There's also a myth that building an AI side hustle requires significant upfront investment. While some tools and platforms do have costs, many successful AI businesses start with minimal investment, using free or low-cost tools initially and reinvesting earnings into better resources as they grow. The key is starting with what you have and scaling intelligently.

Perhaps the most dangerous myth is that you need to quit your job to build a successful AI business. The reality is that many successful AI entrepreneurs built their businesses while maintaining full-time employment. The key is setting realistic expectations and using AI strategically to enhance your productivity and impact. Your goal isn't to create a second full-time job – it's to build systems that leverage both AI and your expertise effectively.

Understanding these realities helps you approach your AI side hustle with clear eyes and realistic expectations. Success comes not from chasing myths about AI magic, but from thoughtfully combining AI capabilities with sound business principles and your unique expertise.

## Your Action Plan

Now that we've covered the landscape, opportunities, and realities of AI side hustles, it's time to turn this knowledge into action. Your journey starts with three key steps that will set you up for success.

First, assess your current situation. Take stock of your available time, existing skills, and resources. Be honest about how many hours you can consistently dedicate each week. Look at your professional experience and identify transferable skills that could give you an advantage in specific niches. Consider what initial resources you have available for tools and learning. Most importantly, think about where your expertise could be most effectively amplified by AI capabilities.

Next, choose your focus. Based on your assessment, select one of the three approaches we discussed – service-based, product-based, or hybrid. Remember, the best choice isn't necessarily the most profitable on paper, but the one that best matches your situation and goals. Consider how each model would allow you to leverage both AI capabilities and your personal expertise. Start with a single, well-defined offering rather than trying to do everything at once.

Finally, create your implementation timeline. Break down your first month into weekly goals. Your first week might focus on understanding your chosen AI tools and how they can enhance your expertise. Week two could involve designing your service delivery process or product framework, focusing on where AI creates the most leverage. Week three might concentrate on building your quality control systems and testing your workflows. Week four could focus on preparing for your first client or launch, ensuring all your systems work together effectively.

The key to this action plan is progressive improvement. You don't need to build everything perfectly from the start. Begin with a minimal viable version of your business that effectively combines AI capabilities with your expertise. Then improve and expand based on real feedback and experience. This approach allows you to start making progress while maintaining your current commitments.

As you move forward, keep referring back to the building blocks we discussed. Each step you take should strengthen your foundation in leveraging AI, acquiring customers, ensuring quality, or managing risk. Focus on building sustainable systems that combine technology and human insight effectively rather than looking for quick wins.

Remember, the goal isn't to create more work for yourself – it's to build a system that can grow and improve over time while fitting into your existing life. Take action, but take it strategically, always looking for ways to create leverage through the thoughtful combination of AI capabilities and your unique expertise.

### ACTION ITEMS

- [ ] Evaluate how many hours you can realistically dedicate each week to building your AI side hustle
- [ ] Identify which business model (service, product, or hybrid) aligns best with your skills and available time
- [ ] Create a 30-day roadmap with specific weekly goals and milestones
- [ ] Determine the AI tools or platforms you need to learn or set up right away
- [ ] Establish simple metrics to measure your early progress and validate your initial approach
- [ ] Plan for at least one real-world test or pilot project to gather honest feedback
- [ ] Schedule a midpoint review to revisit your goals and make necessary adjustments

## Chapter Summary

In this chapter, we've explored the fundamentals of building an AI-powered side hustle in 2025. We've seen how the AI landscape has matured from its early days into a more stable, predictable environment that offers real opportunities for side hustlers. The key isn't just in the technology itself, but in how it can be leveraged to create sustainable, part-time businesses that complement your existing career.

We've examined three main approaches to AI side hustles – service-based, product-based, and hybrid models – each offering different ways to combine AI capabilities with human expertise. We've seen how successful entrepreneurs aren't just automating tasks, but creating strategic systems that multiply their impact while maintaining the crucial human elements that clients value.

The building blocks we've discussed – from leverage frameworks to quality control systems – provide a foundation for creating a sustainable business. Remember that success in this space isn't about replacing human effort with AI, but about finding the right balance between technological capability and personal expertise. It's about building systems that amplify your impact while working within your available time and resources.

As we move into the next chapter, we'll dive deeper into the essential AI tools and technologies that will form your technical foundation. You'll learn how to select, set up, and optimize these tools to support your chosen business model. More importantly, you'll learn how to use them strategically to enhance rather than replace your expertise.

The opportunity is real, but success requires a thoughtful approach. Start small, build systematically, and focus on creating sustainable value. Your next step awaits in Chapter 2.

> **KEY TAKEAWAYS**
>
> - The 2025 AI landscape offers unique advantages: mature tools, stable pricing, and validated business models
> - Success in AI side hustles comes from understanding the fundamental shift from trading time for money to building leveraged systems
> - Your competitive edge lies in combining AI automation with human expertise, not in trying to automate everything
> - The three proven business models (service, product, hybrid) each offer different ways to create leverage while maintaining a full-time job
> - Starting requires minimal resources: focus on strategic time investment, business thinking, and process design rather than technical skills
> - Essential building blocks include your leverage framework, customer acquisition system, value-based pricing, and quality control
> - Common myths about needing technical expertise or huge investments often hold people back - the reality is much more accessible
> - The key to sustainable growth is progressive improvement: start small, validate your approach, and expand based on real feedback

CHAPTER 2

# Essential AI Tools & Setup

The difference between a struggling side hustle and a thriving AI business often comes down to one thing: your tools and how you use them. In the previous chapter, we explored the opportunities in AI side hustles. Now it's time to look at the practical foundation that makes those opportunities achievable.

Think of your AI tool stack as the foundation of your business. Just as a house needs solid foundations to support everything built on top, your AI side hustle needs a robust technical foundation to support its operations. Unlike traditional businesses that might require expensive enterprise software or complex technical infrastructure, AI side hustles can be built with remarkably accessible tools.

What matters most is understanding not just which tools to use, but how to combine them effectively to amplify your impact. In this chapter, we'll explore the essential components of a successful AI business setup, from core AI platforms to automation tools and quality control systems. More importantly, you'll learn how to build a tool system that works while you sleep, scales as you grow, and fits within your budget.

## Understanding AI Platforms

The foundation of any AI side hustle starts with choosing the right AI platforms. But rather than focusing on specific platforms that might change over time, let's understand the fundamental categories and capabilities you need to consider.

At their core, AI platforms fall into two main categories: general-purpose language models and specialized AI tools. General-purpose models are like Swiss Army knives – they can handle a wide range of tasks, from writing and analysis to creative work and problem-solving. These platforms form the backbone of many AI businesses, providing the flexible intelligence needed to handle diverse challenges.

Specialized AI tools, on the other hand, excel at specific tasks. These might include image generation, voice synthesis, data analysis, or code generation. While they have a narrower focus, they often outperform general-purpose models in their specific domains.

When evaluating AI platforms, several key features deserve your attention. First, consider reliability and uptime – your business needs tools that work consistently. Look at response times and processing capabilities – speed matters when you're building automated systems. Examine their ability to handle your expected workload, and understand their pricing models to ensure they fit your budget.

But perhaps most importantly, evaluate how well different platforms can integrate with each other and with your automation tools. The most powerful AI setup isn't a collection of isolated tools, but rather an interconnected system where each component enhances the others.

### ACTION ITEMS

- ☐ Browse 2-3 general-purpose AI platforms to understand their capabilities
- ☐ Look at examples of specialized AI tools (image, voice, code, etc.)
- ☐ Compare free vs paid tiers of popular AI platforms
- ☐ Note which platforms offer good documentation and learning resources
- ☐ Start a list of questions about AI capabilities you want to learn more about

## Automation Tools

While AI platforms provide the intelligence for your business, automation tools provide the infrastructure that makes it scalable. These tools are what transform manual processes into automated workflows, allowing your business to operate efficiently even when you're focused on your day job.

Integration platforms serve as the connective tissue of your automation system. They allow different tools to communicate and work together, creating workflows that can handle complex business processes automatically. These platforms use visual interfaces to connect different services, trigger actions based on specific events, and move data between systems without requiring any coding knowledge.

No-code automation tools take this accessibility even further. They allow you to build sophisticated business processes through simple drag-and-drop interfaces. Whether you're creating customer onboarding sequences, setting up content delivery systems, or building quality control workflows, these tools make it possible to automate complex operations without technical expertise.

Browser extensions and task automation tools add another layer of efficiency. They can handle repetitive tasks directly in your web browser, automate data entry, and streamline common operations. When combined with AI platforms, they can create powerful workflows that handle everything from initial customer contact to final delivery.

The key to successful automation isn't just using these tools – it's using them strategically. Start by identifying your most time-consuming repetitive tasks. These are prime candidates for automation. Then, look for ways to connect different tools to create seamless workflows. The goal is to build systems that can handle routine operations independently, freeing you to focus on strategy and growth.

> **ACTION ITEMS**
>
> - ☐ Watch 1-2 demos of no-code automation platforms
> - ☐ List examples of tasks you've seen automated in other businesses
> - ☐ Research what "workflow automation" means in practice
> - ☐ Look up common automation tools and their basic features
> - ☐ Start noticing repetitive tasks in your daily work

## Business Infrastructure

Beyond AI and automation tools, every successful side hustle needs solid business infrastructure. These are the foundational tools that keep your operation running smoothly and professionally.

Project management tools help you track tasks, deadlines, and workflows. They become especially important as your business grows and you're juggling multiple clients or projects. Look for tools that can integrate with your automation systems, allowing tasks to be created, updated, and completed automatically based on trigger events.

Communication platforms need to be reliable and professional. This includes email systems, messaging platforms, and possibly video conferencing tools. The key is choosing platforms that can be integrated into your automated workflows while maintaining a professional appearance to clients.

File management systems are crucial for organizing and securing your business assets. This includes document storage, version control, and backup systems. Consider how these systems can be automated – for example, automatically organizing files, backing up data, and managing access permissions.

Payment processing might seem straightforward, but it's worth careful consideration. Look for systems that can handle automated billing, recurring payments, and multiple payment methods. The

# THE AI SIDE HUSTLE REVOLUTION

goal is to make it as easy as possible for clients to pay you while minimizing the time you spend on financial administration.

These tools shouldn't exist in isolation. Your project management system should automatically update when AI tasks complete. Your communication platforms should trigger appropriate workflows. Your file management should organize outputs automatically. The goal is to create a seamless system where each piece supports the others.

### ACTION ITEMS

- ☐ Learn what basic tools other online businesses use
- ☐ Research free vs paid options for business tools
- ☐ Understand what "cloud storage" means for a business
- ☐ Look up common payment processing services
- ☐ Start a list of tools you already know how to use

## Setting Up Your Tech Stack

With an understanding of the available tools, let's focus on how to put them together effectively. Setting up your tech stack isn't just about choosing individual tools – it's about creating a cohesive system that works together seamlessly.

Start with your core AI platform. This will be the engine that powers your main business operations. Set up your account, familiarize yourself with the interface, and understand the basic API capabilities if you plan to use them. Pay particular attention to authentication and security settings – these are crucial for protecting your business operations.

Next, establish your automation foundation. Choose an integration platform that can connect with both your AI tools and your business infrastructure. Set up your account and learn the basic workflow creation process. Start simple – you can always add complexity later as your needs grow.

Security should be a priority from day one. Set up two-factor authentication wherever available. Create separate business accounts rather than using personal ones. Implement a password management system to maintain strong, unique passwords for all your tools. Remember, you're building a professional operation, and security needs to be treated accordingly.

Backup systems are equally crucial. Set up automatic backups for all important business data. This includes customer information, business documents, and automation workflows. Consider having redundant systems for critical operations – if one tool goes down, you should have a backup ready to go.

---

**ACTION ITEMS**

- ☐ Learn what 2FA means and why it matters
- ☐ Research basic password management options
- ☐ Understand what "backup" means for digital businesses
- ☐ Learn about business vs personal accounts
- ☐ Read about basic online security practices

---

## Building Your Workflows

Now comes the exciting part – building the automated workflows that will power your business. This is where your tool stack comes to life, creating systems that can operate with minimal intervention.

Start with a simple, core workflow. This might be your main service delivery process or your customer onboarding sequence. Map out each step, identifying where AI needs to be applied and what data needs to move between systems. Build this workflow in your automation platform, testing each step thoroughly before moving on.

When connecting tools together, focus on error handling and reliability. What happens if one step fails? How will you be notified? Build in safeguards and notification systems so you can quickly identify and address any issues that arise.

Testing is crucial. Start with small test cases before handling real client work. Create sample data and run it through your entire workflow. Look for edge cases and potential failure points. It's better to find and fix issues during testing than to discover them with real client work.

Common workflow patterns you might implement include customer inquiry handling and qualification, where AI automatically screens and responds to initial inquiries. Service delivery automation coordinates multiple AI tools to deliver finished products efficiently. Quality control processes combine automated checks with strategic human review points. Follow-up systems gather feedback and maintain client relationships automatically, while payment processing handles billing and invoicing without manual intervention.

The key is to start simple and add complexity gradually as needed. Your workflows will evolve as you learn what works best for your specific business needs.

> **ACTION ITEMS**
>
> ☐ Learn what a "business workflow" means
> ☐ Look up examples of simple automated workflows
> ☐ Understand what "integration" means between tools
> ☐ Research how businesses handle errors in automation
> ☐ Learn what "testing" means in automation

### Quality Control Systems

Quality control is perhaps the most critical aspect of running an AI-powered business. While AI tools can produce work quickly, maintaining consistent quality requires thoughtful systems and processes.

A robust quality control system operates on multiple levels. Automated tools scan AI outputs for basic issues like grammar, formatting, and consistency, catching obvious errors early. Pattern matching and validation ensure outputs meet predetermined criteria and basic quality standards. Strategic quality control – checking that outputs align with business goals and client requirements – typically requires human oversight, but your workflow should focus this attention only on high-level decisions.

Build your quality control workflow to be proactive rather than reactive. Set up systems to catch issues early in the process, before they reach clients. Implement automatic alerts for potential quality issues, and create clear escalation paths for handling problems when they arise.

For example, a content creation workflow might include automated checks for grammar and formatting, verification that content matches the brief and requirements, and strategic review of messaging and brand alignment. This multi-layered approach ensures quality while maintaining efficiency.

### ACTION ITEMS

- [ ] Research how AI outputs can vary in quality
- [ ] Learn about basic quality control methods
- [ ] Understand the difference between automated and human review
- [ ] Look up examples of quality issues in AI outputs
- [ ] Learn what "quality standards" means for digital products

## Cost & Performance Management

Managing costs and performance in an AI-powered business requires careful attention to both technical and financial metrics. Understanding how to optimize these aspects can mean the difference between a profitable operation and one that burns through resources unnecessarily.

Most AI platforms use consumption-based pricing models – you pay for what you use. This makes it crucial to monitor your usage patterns and optimize your workflows accordingly. Look for ways to cache common responses, batch similar requests, and minimize unnecessary API calls.

Performance monitoring should focus on both technical and business metrics. Track response times, error rates, and system availability. But also monitor business metrics like customer satisfaction, delivery times, and cost per deliverable. This dual focus helps ensure that technical optimizations actually translate to business improvements.

As you scale, pay attention to how costs grow in relation to revenue. Some costs will scale linearly with usage, while others might have breakpoints where upgraded plans or different tools become more cost-effective. Plan for these transitions and build them into your growth strategy.

### ACTION ITEMS

- Learn how AI platforms typically charge users
- Research what "API calls" means
- Understand basic business metrics
- Look up how other businesses track performance
- Learn about common pricing models for online tools

Now that we've covered the essential components of your AI business foundation, let's turn theory into practice with a concrete implementation plan that will guide you through the setup process step by step.

**Your Implementation Path**

While it's tempting to jump straight into tool setup, successful implementation requires a structured approach. Here's how we'll tackle this in the coming chapters:

First, in Chapter 3, we'll walk through setting up your core AI foundation. You'll learn exactly how to choose and configure your primary AI platform, set up essential automation tools, establish secure access and backup systems, and build your first basic workflow. We'll cover each step in detail, ensuring you have a solid technical foundation to build upon.

Then, in Chapter 4, we'll help you choose between five proven AI business models. You'll learn about AI service arbitrage, custom GPT development, content systems, prompt engineering services, and AI consultation. More importantly, you'll understand which model best fits your skills and circumstances.

In Chapters 5-9, we'll provide detailed implementation guides for each business model. Each chapter will show you exactly how to build, launch, and grow that specific type of AI business. You'll learn the exact steps, systems, and strategies needed for your chosen path.

Finally, Chapters 10 and 11 will cover advanced strategies and business management, showing you how to optimize what you've built and manage it efficiently alongside your day job.

For now, focus on understanding the components we've covered in this chapter. The detailed implementation steps will follow, ensuring you can build your technical foundation confidently and systematically.

**Chapter Summary**

In this chapter, we've explored the essential tools and technical foundation needed to build a successful AI side hustle. We've seen how the right combination of AI platforms, automation tools, and business infrastructure can create a system that works efficiently while you maintain your primary career.

We've examined the key categories of tools you'll need, from general-purpose AI models to specialized solutions, and how to

# THE AI SIDE HUSTLE REVOLUTION

evaluate them based on reliability, integration capabilities, and cost-effectiveness. We've also explored how automation tools can transform manual processes into scalable workflows, and how proper business infrastructure supports sustainable growth.

The focus has been on building a practical, efficient foundation rather than an overly complex system. We've emphasized the importance of starting with essential components and growing your tool stack strategically as your business evolves. Quality control and security have been highlighted as crucial elements to implement from the beginning.

As we move into the next chapter, we'll explore how to use this technical foundation to implement specific business models. You'll learn how to leverage these tools effectively to create value for clients while maintaining the efficiency that makes a side hustle sustainable.

### KEY TAKEAWAYS

- Choose AI platforms based on reliability, integration capabilities, and cost-effectiveness rather than just features
- Automation tools are crucial for scaling your business while maintaining your day job
- Build a cohesive system where tools work together rather than isolated solutions
- Start with essential components and grow your tech stack strategically
- Implement quality control and security measures from the beginning
- Focus on reliability and efficiency over complexity
- Your tool selection should support your specific business model and work style
- Plan for scalability but start with a minimum viable setup

CHAPTER 3

# Setting Up Your Technical Foundation

Before diving into specific AI business models, you need a reliable workspace for experimenting with and learning from AI. This doesn't mean complex infrastructure - it means having the right tools set up properly, staying organized, and protecting your work.

## Your AI Workspace

Your primary AI platform will be where you spend most of your time experimenting and developing ideas. ChatGPT Plus provides GPT-4 access through a web interface for $20 per month. The cost is fixed and predictable, and the interface is straightforward: log in, type your prompt, get your response.

Claude offers an alternative approach. It has a free tier for basic use, but expect to pay based on usage if you're doing serious work. It handles longer content well and offers some unique capabilities, but requires more attention to usage tracking and cost management.

Start with a dedicated account for your AI work, separate from any personal AI use. This separation helps you:

- Track costs accurately
- Keep your experiments organized
- Maintain clear records of what works

Don't worry about API access yet. While APIs offer more possibilities, they add complexity and costs you don't need when starting out. Focus first on learning what AI can and can't do through the standard interface.

Store your prompts and results systematically from the start. A simple text file or Google Doc works fine - just make sure you record:

- What you tried
- What worked
- What failed
- Ideas for improvement

> **ACTION ITEMS**
>
> ☐ Create a dedicated email address for your AI business accounts
> ☐ Sign up for your chosen AI platform (from Chapter 2)
> ☐ Create a document titled "AI Experiments Log"
> ☐ Write your first test prompt (a simple writing task)
> ☐ Record the results and your observations

### Organization & Storage

Good organization makes the difference between useful experiments and wasted time. Create a simple but clear file structure from the start. You need space for your prompts, results, and ideas.

Set up three main folders in Google Drive or your preferred storage:

Your Prompts folder stores the instructions you give to AI. Create subfolders by purpose - writing prompts, analysis prompts, generation prompts. When a prompt works well, save it with notes about why it worked.

Your Results folder keeps the AI outputs worth saving. Don't save everything - focus on successful results and interesting failures. Add notes about what made them work or fail.

# THE AI SIDE HUSTLE REVOLUTION

Your Ideas folder tracks potential projects and improvements. When you spot a possible use for AI, write it down with any relevant prompts or results.

Version tracking doesn't need to be complex. Date your files (YYYY-MM-DD) and keep old versions that worked well. Delete experiments that failed unless they taught you something specific.

Back up your work regularly. Export your best prompts and results weekly. Store them somewhere separate from your main working space. A simple USB drive works fine for this.

### ACTION ITEMS

- [ ] Create three main folders: Prompts, Results, and Ideas
- [ ] Set up a basic file naming system (YYYY-MM-DD-description)
- [ ] Set up a free Google Drive or Dropbox account for cloud storage
- [ ] Schedule a weekly Friday backup reminder
- [ ] Save your first test prompt and result using your naming system

### Testing & Iteration

Testing AI isn't like testing normal software. You're looking for reliability and consistency in the outputs. Start with simple tests: give the same prompt multiple times and compare the results. Note where responses vary and why.

Keep a testing document for each type of task you try. Record:

- The exact prompt used
- What you expected
- What you got
- Any patterns in the responses
- Ideas for improvements

When something works well, try breaking it. Change small parts of successful prompts to understand what makes them work. Test with different:

- Lengths of input
- Types of requests
- Writing styles
- Formatting requirements

Learn from failures - they often teach more than successes. When a prompt fails, try to understand why before moving on. Was it too vague? Too specific? Missing key context? These insights improve your next attempts.

Don't get stuck endlessly tweaking. If a prompt works reliably for your needs, save it and move on. You can always improve it later when you have a specific reason to do so.

### ACTION ITEMS

- ☐ Pick a simple writing task (like "write a product description")
- ☐ Create a testing template with sections for prompt, result, and notes
- ☐ Run your test prompt 3 times in a row
- ☐ Write down what's different in each response
- ☐ List 3 ways to improve your prompt

## Protection & Costs

Keep your work secure with basic precautions. Use a password manager for strong, unique passwords on your AI platform and storage accounts. Enable two-factor authentication where available. Keep your business account separate from personal use.

Track your AI platform costs weekly. ChatGPT Plus is straightforward at $20 monthly. For usage-based platforms like

Claude, set up spending alerts and log your usage until you understand your patterns. This tracking helps you plan your experiments and manage your budget effectively.

Back up your work regularly:

- Export your prompt library weekly
- Save successful results
- Protect your testing notes
- Store backups in two places

Don't overcomplicate security or backup systems. Simple precautions, consistently applied, prevent most common problems. Focus on protecting your most valuable assets: your proven prompts and test results.

Remember: you're building a foundation for experimenting with AI business models. Keep your setup simple but reliable. You can always add more sophisticated tools and processes when you have a specific need for them.

For now, focus on building your first consultation framework. The businesses struggling with AI implementation need your systematic approach more than they realize. Your opportunity is helping them bridge the gap between AI possibilities and practical business results.

## Chapter Summary

In this chapter, we've explored how to set up a professional and efficient technical foundation for your AI side hustle. We've covered the essential components of a reliable workspace, from choosing and configuring your primary AI platform to establishing proper organization and security measures.

We've examined the practical considerations of different AI platforms, understanding their costs, capabilities, and best use cases. We've also explored the importance of proper organization, file management, and backup systems that will support your business as it grows. Security and cost management have been emphasized as crucial elements of a sustainable operation.

The focus has been on building a professional yet practical setup that supports your business goals without unnecessary complexity. We've emphasized the importance of separating business and personal use, maintaining clear records, and establishing systems that scale efficiently.

As we move into the next chapter, we'll explore specific AI business models and how to leverage this technical foundation to create value for clients. You'll learn how to apply these tools and systems to build a thriving AI side hustle that complements your existing career.

### KEY TAKEAWAYS

- Set up dedicated business accounts for AI platforms to maintain professional standards and track costs
- Choose AI platforms based on your specific needs, considering both capabilities and cost structures
- Implement proper organization and file management from the start to support future growth
- Establish robust backup and security measures to protect your business assets
- Track experiments and results systematically to build on what works
- Separate business and personal use to maintain clear records and professional boundaries
- Start with essential tools and expand based on actual business needs
- Focus on building systems that scale efficiently as your business grows

CHAPTER 4

# Five Proven AI Business Models

Now that you have a solid technical foundation in place from Chapter 3, it's time to explore the business models that will help you monetize these capabilities. While new applications of AI emerge daily, five business models have consistently proven themselves effective for entrepreneurs building around their full-time jobs. These aren't theoretical possibilities or experimental approaches – they're working right now, generating real income for people just like you.

What makes these models particularly valuable is their ability to leverage both the automation advantage we discussed in Chapter 1 and the technical foundation we built in Chapter 3. Each model allows you to build systems that can operate efficiently with limited time investment. Whether you're drawn to service delivery, product creation, or consulting, these models provide frameworks for building sustainable income streams without sacrificing your primary career.

In this chapter, we'll explore each model in detail, examining not just how they work, but what makes them successful and how to implement them effectively using your established AI foundation. More importantly, you'll learn how to choose the right model for your specific situation. After all, the best business model isn't necessarily the most profitable on paper – it's the one that aligns with your skills, resources, and goals.

Let's begin with perhaps the most accessible entry point into the world of AI side hustles.

## AI Service Arbitrage

Among the five proven models, AI service arbitrage stands out as perhaps the most accessible entry point into AI side hustles. At its core, this model is about becoming the intelligent bridge between powerful AI capabilities and clients who need specific results. While anyone can access AI tools, most businesses lack the time, expertise, or inclination to use them effectively.

Think of it like being a skilled chef in a kitchen full of advanced cooking equipment. While anyone could theoretically access the same tools, your expertise in using them effectively, combined with your systems for consistent delivery, creates real value for clients who just want excellent meals without learning to cook themselves.

The beauty of this model lies in its simplicity: clients pay for outcomes, not tools. By mastering AI platforms and building efficient delivery systems, you can provide valuable services while maintaining healthy margins through automation. Whether it's content creation, market research, data analysis, or social media management, the key is building systems that deliver consistent, high-quality results with minimal manual intervention.

The setup requirements are surprisingly modest. You'll need access to relevant AI platforms, some basic automation tools for workflow management, and quality control systems. But the real investment is in developing your processes – creating workflows that maintain quality standards, scale with demand, and deliver predictable outcomes time after time.

> **ACTION ITEMS**
>
> ☐ List 3 services you could deliver using your current AI skills
> ☐ Write down your available hours per week for service delivery
> ☐ Identify one repetitive task you could automate
> ☐ Research 2-3 competitors offering similar AI services
> ☐ Outline a basic workflow for your chosen service

### Custom GPT Development

While general-purpose AI models are powerful, a growing opportunity lies in creating specialized GPTs that solve specific business problems. This second proven model focuses on developing, optimizing, and monetizing custom GPTs that serve particular industries or address unique business challenges.

The opportunity here stems from a fundamental market reality: while anyone can access ChatGPT, not everyone can create a specialized GPT that truly serves a specific business need. Consider a real estate agent who needs to write compelling property listings, or a consultant who regularly generates client proposals. These professionals don't want a general AI tool – they want something that understands their industry, speaks their language, and delivers exactly what they need.

What makes this model particularly attractive for side hustlers is its accessibility. Creating a custom GPT doesn't require coding skills or deep technical expertise. Instead, success comes from understanding specific industry needs and crafting effective solutions. The development process focuses on creating clear instructions, building comprehensive knowledge bases, and optimizing performance for specific use cases.

Monetization in this space takes various forms. Some developers sell direct access to their specialized GPTs, while others create subscription-based services. Many successful entrepreneurs in this space build suites of related GPTs, serving different aspects of the same industry. The key is focusing on specific value delivery – solving real problems for defined audiences rather than trying to create generic solutions.

> **ACTION ITEMS**
>
> ☐ List 3 industries you know well enough to serve
> ☐ Identify specific problems these industries face
> ☐ Research if GPTs already exist for these problems
> ☐ Write down one specific task a GPT could help with
> ☐ Outline the basic features your GPT would need

While custom GPTs focus on specialized tools, our next model takes a broader approach to solving business challenges.

### AI-Powered Content Systems

The third model moves beyond simple content creation to build comprehensive systems that can handle entire content operations automatically. This approach addresses one of the most persistent challenges businesses face: maintaining consistent, high-quality content across multiple channels.

Think of an AI-powered content system as a digital publishing house that runs largely on autopilot. It's not just about generating blog posts or social media updates – it's about creating an entire ecosystem that handles everything from initial content planning to final distribution and performance tracking.

What sets successful content systems apart is their ability to maintain quality at scale. This involves building sophisticated workflows that combine AI generation with strategic human oversight. The best systems know when to leverage AI for heavy lifting and when to incorporate human expertise for refinement and strategy.

Client management becomes particularly important in this model. The key is setting clear expectations from the start about what the system can and cannot do. Successful operators develop clear processes for client input, approval points, and revision requests. They also create comprehensive reporting systems that demonstrate the value being delivered.

### ACTION ITEMS

- ☐ List types of content you're comfortable creating
- ☐ Identify potential automation points in content creation
- ☐ Write down your quality standards for content
- ☐ Outline a basic content approval workflow
- ☐ List 3 ways to measure content system success

## Prompt Engineering Services

As businesses dive deeper into AI implementation, they're discovering a crucial truth: the difference between mediocre and exceptional AI results often lies in how you communicate with the AI. This realization has created a growing demand for prompt engineering expertise, opening up our fourth proven business model.

Prompt engineering services might sound technical, but at their heart, they're about helping clients get better results from their AI investments. Think of a prompt engineer as an AI whisperer – someone who knows how to speak the language of AI models to get consistently superior outputs. This role has become increasingly valuable as businesses realize that simply having access to AI tools isn't enough; knowing how to use them effectively is what creates real value.

What makes this model particularly attractive for side hustlers is its natural scalability. Many aspects of prompt engineering can be systematized and templated, allowing you to serve multiple clients efficiently. You might start by analyzing a client's current AI usage, develop a custom prompt library for their specific needs, and then create workflow templates that their team can follow. The initial work can often be repurposed and adapted for similar clients in the same industry.

The value proposition is straightforward and compelling: better prompts mean better results, saved time, and reduced AI costs. Clients often see immediate improvements in their AI outputs, making it easy to demonstrate ROI. This tangible value makes it easier to justify professional fees and build long-term client relationships.

Education plays a crucial role in this model. Many clients initially don't understand why prompt engineering matters or how it can impact their results. Successful prompt engineering services often include a significant educational component, helping clients understand not just what works, but why it works. This education process frequently leads to longer-term engagements and referrals.

### ACTION ITEMS

- ☐ Write down your current prompt engineering experience
- ☐ List 3 ways you've improved AI outputs
- ☐ Identify industries that could benefit from better prompts
- ☐ Outline a basic prompt testing process
- ☐ Draft a simple explanation of why prompts matter

## AI Business Consultation

Our fifth proven model addresses a growing need in the market: helping businesses understand and implement AI effectively. As artificial intelligence becomes more central to business operations, many companies – especially small and medium-sized businesses

– find themselves needing guidance on how to leverage these technologies effectively.

What makes AI consultation particularly viable as a side hustle is that you don't need to be a technical expert or programmer. Instead, success comes from understanding both business processes and AI capabilities, then helping clients bridge that gap. It's about being the practical guide who can translate AI possibilities into business realities.

The most successful AI consultants don't try to serve everyone. Instead, they focus on specific industries or use cases where they can deliver the most value. For example, a consultant might help real estate agencies automate their property listing descriptions, follow-up emails, and market analysis reports. Another might focus on helping law firms implement AI for contract review and legal research. Some consultants specialize in helping small e-commerce businesses set up AI customer service systems and automated product description generators.

The key to making this work alongside a full-time job is developing systematic approaches that can be replicated across clients. Rather than reinventing the wheel for each consultation, successful consultants create structured programs and methodologies. For instance, you might develop a standard "AI Readiness Assessment" that helps identify a client's most promising automation opportunities. Or you could create an "AI Implementation Roadmap" template that guides clients through the process of selecting tools, training staff, and measuring results.

Knowledge building becomes an ongoing part of the business. Successful AI consultants stay current with AI capabilities and applications, but more importantly, they develop a deep understanding of how these technologies can solve real business problems. A consultant working with restaurants might learn how AI can optimize menu planning, inventory management, and staff scheduling. Someone focusing on professional services might become expert in using AI for proposal writing, project management, and client reporting.

> **ACTION ITEMS**
>
> ☐ List your current areas of business expertise
> ☐ Identify which AI tools you know well enough to teach
> ☐ Write down 3 common business problems AI could solve
> ☐ Outline a basic consultation process
> ☐ List your current professional network connections

## Model Selection Framework

Now that we've explored each model in detail, you might be wondering which one is right for you. The answer isn't always obvious, and it's not just about choosing the most profitable option. Success often comes from selecting the model that best fits your current circumstances, skills, and goals.

Let's start with time availability, often the most crucial factor for side hustlers. AI service arbitrage, once set up, can run with minimal daily intervention. The systems you build handle most of the work, requiring only periodic oversight and quality control. Custom GPT development, on the other hand, demands more concentrated effort upfront but can become quite passive once your products are launched and stable.

Content systems fall somewhere in the middle – they need regular attention but can be highly automated with good systems in place. Prompt engineering services offer flexibility; you can often schedule client work around your other commitments. AI consultation typically requires the most dedicated time blocks, though even this can be systematized to some degree.

Technical skills play a different role in each model. Don't let this factor intimidate you – none of these models require programming expertise. Instead, think about your comfort level with technology and your willingness to learn new tools. Service arbitrage needs basic tool familiarity, while custom GPT development requires a deeper understanding of AI capabilities. Content systems demand strong process design skills, and prompt engineering requires detailed understanding of how AI models work.

Initial investment varies significantly between models. Service arbitrage and prompt engineering can start with minimal investment – mainly just subscriptions to key AI tools. Content systems might require a more robust tool stack, while consultation focuses more on knowledge building than tool investment. Custom GPT development often falls somewhere in the middle, with costs varying based on your approach.

The scalability of each model also deserves careful consideration. Service arbitrage and content systems can scale well with automation. Custom GPTs offer excellent scalability once created, as they can be sold repeatedly with minimal additional effort. Prompt engineering and consultation services typically require more direct involvement but can be productized to some degree through templates and systematic approaches.

### ACTION ITEMS

- ☐ Write down your weekly available hours
- ☐ List your current technical skills and comfort level
- ☐ Calculate your available startup budget
- ☐ Rate your interest in each business model (1-5)
- ☐ Identify your preferred working style (hands-on vs automated)

## Combining Business Models

While each of these models can succeed independently, some of the most successful AI side hustlers have discovered the power of combining multiple approaches. This isn't about trying to do everything at once – rather, it's about recognizing the natural synergies between different models and leveraging them strategically.

Consider how these models naturally complement each other. A content system client might realize they need help crafting better prompts, leading to prompt engineering opportunities. An AI consultation client might need a custom GPT for their specific industry. These natural connections allow you to expand your services organically, following client needs rather than forcing growth.

The efficiency gains from combining models can be substantial. Many of the tools and systems you build for one service can support others. The automation workflows you create for content delivery might adapt perfectly for other services. The knowledge you gain serving one type of client often transfers directly to other offerings. This shared infrastructure makes each additional service more profitable than if you were starting from scratch.

This approach also helps manage risk. Different services often appeal to different market segments or serve different needs within the same market. This diversity can provide stability – if demand for one service dips, others can help maintain your income. It also gives you multiple paths to grow your business, allowing you to focus more energy on whatever is working best at any given time.

The key to successfully combining models is to expand thoughtfully and systematically. Start with one model and master it. Build solid systems and establish a stable client base. Then look for natural opportunities to add complementary services. Let your existing clients guide you – their needs and requests often point the way to logical expansions.

Think of it like building with Lego blocks. You start with a solid foundation piece, then add compatible pieces that enhance and strengthen your structure. Each addition should connect naturally with what you've already built, creating a more robust and valuable whole.

## ACTION ITEMS

- ☐ Choose your primary business model to start with
- ☐ List potential complementary services
- ☐ Identify shared tools or systems you could use
- ☐ Write down your 90-day focus plan
- ☐ Set 3 specific goals for your first month

## Chapter Summary

In this chapter, we've explored five proven AI business models that have consistently demonstrated their effectiveness for entrepreneurs building alongside their full-time careers. We've examined how each model leverages AI capabilities differently, from the accessible entry point of service arbitrage to the strategic depth of AI consultation.

We've seen how these models can be adapted to different skill sets, time commitments, and goals. The focus has been on understanding not just how each model works, but what makes it successful and how it can be implemented effectively using your established AI foundation.

Most importantly, we've provided a framework for choosing the right model for your specific situation. Success isn't about picking the most profitable model on paper – it's about finding the approach that aligns with your skills, resources, and circumstances while providing the flexibility needed to maintain your primary career.

As we move into the next chapters, we'll dive deep into implementing each of these models, providing detailed guides for turning these concepts into profitable reality. The foundation you've built in understanding these models will serve as your roadmap for building a sustainable AI side hustle.

## KEY TAKEAWAYS

- Five proven models offer different paths to success: service arbitrage, custom GPT development, content systems, prompt engineering, and consultation
- Choose your model based on your skills, available time, and preferred working style rather than just potential profits
- Each model can be started and operated alongside a full-time career when properly systematized
- Success comes from building efficient systems rather than constant hands-on effort
- Your initial choice isn't permanent - many successful entrepreneurs start with one model and expand over time
- Focus on creating value through expertise and efficient delivery rather than just access to AI tools
- The right model matches your current circumstances while allowing room for growth
- Implementation matters more than model selection - success comes from taking action with the right approach

CHAPTER 5

# AI Service Arbitrage

Imagine a client needs 10 perfect AI-generated images for their new product launch. They could spend hours learning Midjourney, testing dozens of prompts, sorting through hundreds of outputs, and hoping they end up with what they need. Or they could hire you - someone who knows the tools, understands the process, and delivers exactly what they want.

This is AI Service Arbitrage in action. You're not just reselling AI outputs - you're providing a valuable service by handling all the complexity, iteration, and quality control that goes into getting great results from AI tools. While the client gets their 10 perfect images, you might have generated 500 or more to get there, meticulously checking each one for quality issues. Is that hand anatomically correct? Does it have the right number of fingers? Are the left and right hands actually on the correct sides?

And this is just one example of AI Service Arbitrage. The same principles apply whether you're helping clients get perfect research reports from AI analysis tools, polished blog posts from language models, or actionable insights from document processing. In each case, you're the expert who knows how to get reliable, professional results while saving clients time and frustration.

Think of it like being a professional photographer in the AI age. Your clients don't need to know about aperture settings, lighting ratios, or post-processing techniques - they just want great photos. Similarly, your AI service clients don't need to understand prompt engineering, parameter settings, or output refinement - they just want great results that solve their business needs.

> **ACTION ITEMS**
>
> ☐ Write down 3 AI tools you're most comfortable using
> ☐ List 5 common problems these tools could solve
> ☐ Identify your target service price range
> ☐ Calculate how many clients you could handle monthly
> ☐ Write down your unique value proposition

In this chapter, you'll learn how to build your first AI service arbitrage business. We'll start by choosing a service you can offer, set up your tools and workflows, and guide you through getting your first paying client. By the end of your first month, you'll have everything you need to start generating revenue in your spare time.

Let's begin with choosing your first service...

## Choosing Your Service

The key to successful AI service arbitrage isn't just picking a service you can deliver - it's finding one where your time and expertise add clear value. While we used AI image generation as an example, there are several service types that follow the same principle: you handle the complexity and iteration while delivering polished results to your clients.

AI image generation services are perfect for clients who need product visualization, marketing materials, or social media content. Just like our earlier example, you'll spend time perfecting prompts, checking details, and ensuring every image meets professional standards. A client might need product photos for their e-commerce store - you can create consistent, high-quality images that showcase their products in the perfect light, without them needing to understand the intricacies of AI image generation.

Content creation offers similar opportunities. While anyone can ask ChatGPT to write a blog post, delivering professional-quality content requires understanding tone, structure, and context. You might generate multiple versions, fact-check the output, refine the style, and ensure everything aligns with the client's brand voice. The client gets polished, ready-to-publish content without wrestling with prompts or checking for AI hallucinations.

Research services transform raw AI capabilities into actionable insights. Instead of clients spending hours sorting through AI-generated research data, you can deliver focused reports that answer their specific questions. This might involve cross-referencing multiple sources, verifying information, and presenting findings in a clear, professional format.

Document processing services help clients make sense of their existing content. Whether it's analyzing contracts, summarizing reports, or extracting key data, you're not just running documents through AI - you're ensuring accurate, reliable results that clients can trust.

The most profitable services share three crucial elements. First, clients need consistent, quality results they can rely on. Second, the process requires significant iteration and refinement - this is where your expertise becomes valuable. Finally, your quality control and attention to detail add clear value that clients will pay for.

### ACTION ITEMS

- [ ] List 3 services that match your current AI skills
- [ ] Write down your quality standards
- [ ] Identify potential bottlenecks in delivery
- [ ] Plan how you'll differentiate from competitors

Now that you've identified potential services, let's validate that there's a real market for what you want to offer.

## Market Research and Validation

Before diving into setup, let's make sure your chosen service has real market potential. This doesn't require extensive research - just some practical investigation to validate that people will pay for what you're planning to offer.

Start by looking at existing service providers. If you're interested in AI image generation, spend an hour browsing Fiverr and Upwork. Look for sellers offering similar services. Don't be discouraged if you find competition - that's actually a good sign. It means there's an existing market for these services. Pay attention to their service descriptions and client reviews. What are clients praising? What are they complaining about? These insights will help you position your service effectively.

Next, look at where your potential clients are already seeking help. Join Facebook groups or subreddits related to your chosen niche. You'll often find people asking for help with the exact problems your service could solve. For example, e-commerce sellers frequently ask about product photography alternatives, or small business owners seek help with consistent social media content. These are your potential clients.

The key is finding pain points you can solve. When someone posts "I spent three hours trying to get Midjourney to create a decent product image and everything looks wrong," that's an opportunity. When a business owner complains "I tried using ChatGPT for blog posts but they all sound robotic," they're describing a problem you can solve.

Test your service idea with a simple offer. Find a relevant online community and look for someone struggling with a problem you can solve. Offer to help one person for free or at a reduced rate in exchange for feedback. This gives you a real-world test case and helps you understand the practical challenges of delivering your service.

Remember, you're not just selling AI outputs - you're selling solutions to real problems. The most successful arbitrage services solve specific pain points that clients are actively trying to address.

Whether it's saving time, ensuring quality, or delivering consistent results, your service needs to offer clear value.

> **ACTION ITEMS**
>
> ☐ Join 3 relevant online communities
> ☐ Find 5 competitors and analyze their offerings
> ☐ List common client complaints about AI tools
> ☐ Identify underserved client needs

With a validated service and clear understanding of the market, it's time to tackle one of the most crucial decisions: setting your prices.

## Understanding Your Pricing

Setting profitable prices for AI service arbitrage requires understanding both your costs and the value you provide to clients. Let's break this down into a systematic approach that ensures your pricing reflects your true value while remaining competitive.

### VALUE-BASED PRICING PRINCIPLES

The key is remembering that clients aren't paying for direct access to AI tools – they're paying for your expertise in getting the best results from these tools. Consider a typical content arbitrage project where a client needs a technical blog post. While they could spend $20 on ChatGPT Plus and attempt it themselves, they'd likely spend four to five hours learning prompt engineering, generating multiple versions, fact-checking the output, and editing the content into a cohesive piece. For a business owner whose time is worth $100 per hour, that's a $500 investment of time, not counting the frustration of learning the tools.

Your service transforms this experience. You might spend ninety minutes crafting perfect prompts, generating multiple versions, verifying technical accuracy, and polishing the final piece. Your costs include a fraction of your AI tool subscriptions and your time investment. If you charge $299 for the package, you're saving the client significant time and effort while maintaining a healthy profit margin.

This same value proposition applies across different types of AI arbitrage. Whether you're helping clients get perfect AI-generated images, processing documents efficiently, or conducting AI-powered research, your value lies in your ability to get better results faster than clients could achieve on their own.

## CALCULATING YOUR PRICING

Let's walk through a practical example of pricing an AI service package. Start with your direct costs - for a typical project, you might spend about $5 worth of AI tool credits generating the necessary outputs. Then consider your time investment. If you value your time at $50 per hour (a reasonable starting rate) and expect to spend two hours on the project, that's $100 for your expertise. Don't forget to factor in small overhead costs like storage and software subscriptions - perhaps $2 per project.

Experience shows that most projects need some adjustments, so build in a buffer for revisions. A good rule of thumb is adding 30% to your base costs. In our example, that's an extra $32 (30% of your $107 in direct costs) to cover additional work without eating into your profits. This brings your base cost to $139.

This base cost covers your tools, time, and potential revisions, but it doesn't include your profit margin. For a sustainable business that can grow, aim to double your base cost. This brings your target price to $278, which you might round up to $299 for marketing purposes. This pricing structure ensures you're well compensated while still delivering excellent value to your clients.

## PACKAGE STRUCTURE

As your service grows, consider offering different service tiers to accommodate varying client needs and budgets. A basic package might include essential deliverables with limited revisions and standard turnaround times. This entry-level option helps clients test your service with minimal risk.

Your standard package should be your primary offering, including more comprehensive deliverables and additional revision rounds. The faster turnaround time and extra attention justify a higher price point, making this your most profitable option for regular clients.

For clients who need the highest level of service, offer a premium package. This might include maximum deliverables, priority service, and the fastest possible turnaround. While fewer clients will choose this option, it provides excellent value for those with urgent needs or complex projects.

## COMMUNICATING YOUR PRICING

When presenting your pricing to clients, focus on the value you deliver rather than the costs involved. Emphasize the time they'll save by not having to learn complex AI tools or manage quality control themselves. Highlight your professional quality standards and the reliability of your service. Most importantly, focus on the business outcomes they'll achieve - whether that's more professional-looking product images, more engaging content, or more actionable research insights.

Remember that your pricing isn't just about covering costs - it's about providing value that makes your service an investment rather than an expense for your clients. When you can demonstrate how your service helps them achieve their business goals more efficiently, the price becomes secondary to the results you deliver.

> **ACTION ITEMS**
>
> - ☐ Calculate your monthly tool costs
> - ☐ Estimate hours needed per typical project
> - ☐ Set your target hourly rate
> - ☐ Add up fixed costs (subscriptions, software)
> - ☐ Create three service package price points
> - ☐ Track actual time and costs for each project
> - ☐ Refine pricing based on experience
> - ☐ Consider package-specific adjustments

With your service concept and pricing structure defined, it's time to put everything together into a complete service offering and validate it with real-world testing.

### Service Validation and Minimum Viable Service

Before investing significant time in setup, let's validate your complete service package with a simple test run. This isn't just about testing your pricing - it's about proving that you can deliver real value that clients will pay for while maintaining quality and profitability.

Start by creating one sample deliverable for yourself. If you're offering content arbitrage, write a blog post using your planned process. For research arbitrage, compile a market analysis report. For image arbitrage, create a set of product photos. The key is going through your entire workflow, from initial AI generation through quality control and final polish. This serves two purposes: you'll learn the real requirements of delivery, and you'll have a sample to show potential clients.

Let's walk through a research arbitrage example. Choose a common business question - perhaps a market analysis of a growing industry. Begin by breaking down how you'll transform raw AI capabilities into valuable insights. You might discover that while AI tools can gather initial data quickly, the real value comes from your ability to verify information, identify patterns, and present findings in a way that answers your client's specific questions. What starts as a simple prompt like "analyze the electric vehicle market" becomes a carefully crafted series of queries that extract precise, relevant information.

Time yourself through this process. How long does it take to gather initial data, verify key points, and compile everything into a professional report? This helps you validate both your workflow and your pricing assumptions. If you discover that comprehensive research takes six hours instead of three, you'll need to either adjust your process for efficiency or revise your pricing structure to maintain profitability.

Now create your minimum viable service package. Instead of offering general "AI research services," be specific about what clients will receive. For example, you might offer a "7-Day Market Analysis Package" that includes verified industry data, competitor analysis, and actionable recommendations. The key is making your offer concrete enough that clients understand exactly what they're getting, while keeping it manageable enough that you can deliver consistently.

The final validation step is offering this package to one test client at a reduced rate. Be transparent - explain that you're launching this service and offering a discount for initial clients in exchange for feedback. This gives you a real-world test while building your portfolio and testimonials.

Remember, your first service offering doesn't need to be perfect. It needs to be good enough to deliver clear value while giving you room to learn and improve. You can expand and refine your offerings as you better understand what clients need and how to deliver it efficiently using AI tools.

### Service Setup Guide

Let's get practical about exactly what you need to run your service efficiently. We'll cover the essential tools, templates, and systems that make professional delivery possible.

## ESSENTIAL TOOLS AND COSTS

Starting an AI service business doesn't require a huge upfront investment. Your toolkit will vary based on your service type, but here's what you'll need for different specialties:

For image generation services, your core tool will be either Midjourney (\$30/month) or DALL-E (\$20/month). You'll access Midjourney through Discord, while DALL-E has its own interface. Consider adding a basic photo editing tool like Canva (free tier available) for minor adjustments.

Content creation services center around tools like ChatGPT Plus (\$20/month) or Claude (\$20/month). Complement these with Grammarly (free tier available) for proofreading and Copyscape (\$10/month) for plagiarism checking. Consider specialized tools like SurferSEO (\$60/month) only after you have paying clients who need SEO optimization.

Research service providers should focus on tools that verify and organize information. Start with ChatGPT Plus or Claude for initial research, combined with Notion (free tier available) for organizing findings. Add Zotero (free) for reference management if you're handling academic work.

Document processing services might use ChatGPT Plus combined with Adobe Acrobat Reader (free) for PDF handling. Tools like Zapier (free tier available) can help automate document workflows once you're handling larger volumes.

Chatbot development requires access to platforms like ChatGPT API (pay per use) or Claude. Start with a simple development environment like Visual Studio Code (free) and add specialized testing tools only as your client base grows.

Every service type needs basic business tools:

- Google Workspace (\$6/month) for email and document management
- Trello or ClickUp (free tiers available) for project tracking
- PayPal or Stripe (transaction fees only) for payments

Remember, start with minimal tools and expand based on actual client needs and revenue. Many premium tools offer free alternatives that work perfectly well when you're starting out. Focus on mastering a few essential tools rather than spreading yourself thin across many platforms.

> **ACTION ITEMS**
>
> ☐ Set up accounts for your core AI tools
> ☐ Create templates for client communication
> ☐ Set up a basic project management system
> ☐ Establish your file organization structure
> ☐ Test your workflow with a sample project

## BASIC WORKFLOW TEMPLATES

Your service needs three core workflows that guide every client project from start to finish. Let's look at how each one works.

The client onboarding workflow begins with your initial response to an inquiry, where you'll explain your service and collect the client's requirements. Once you've confirmed the project scope, you'll handle payment processing and kick off the actual work. Having this structured approach ensures you gather all necessary information upfront and set clear expectations.

Your service delivery workflow is where the real work happens. Following the quality control system outlined earlier, you'll start with a thorough review of client requirements, move through the creation phase with ongoing quality checks, and complete a final review before delivery. This systematic approach ensures consistent, professional results.

The project completion workflow is crucial for building long-term success. After confirming successful delivery, collect feedback about the experience. This is also the perfect time to request a testimonial if the client is happy with your work. Consider whether there's an opportunity for additional services or referrals, and finally, archive the project properly for future reference.

Track each client's progress through these workflows using a simple document or spreadsheet. This helps you stay organized and ensures nothing falls through the cracks, even as you take on more clients.

> **ACTION ITEMS**
>
> ☐ Create a client onboarding workflow
> ☐ Set up a project tracking system
> ☐ Develop a quality control checklist
> ☐ Write a project completion workflow
> ☐ Test your workflows with a sample project

## QUALITY CONTROL SYSTEM

Quality control isn't just a final checklist - it's a system that runs throughout your entire process. Think of it as three distinct phases, each building on the last to ensure professional results.

The initial review happens when you first receive client requirements. Before you generate a single image or start any work, carefully review everything the client has provided. Are their reference images clear enough to work from? Do their brand guidelines include all necessary color codes? Have they specified all required angles or views? Catching missing information here prevents costly revisions later.

During the creation phase, implement rapid quality checks as you work. For image generation, this means watching for common AI issues like anatomical errors or inconsistent lighting while you're still in the generation phase. When writing content, it means checking facts and tone as you go. These quick assessments help you adjust your approach early, saving hours of revision time.

The final quality review is your most comprehensive check. Look at technical elements first - resolution, clarity, and any service-specific technical requirements. Then verify accuracy against the client's brief - does every element match what they requested? Finally, assess the overall professional polish. Would you be proud to showcase this in your portfolio? Does it meet commercial standards?

Keep a record of quality issues you discover and how you resolved them. This growing knowledge base helps you prevent similar issues in future projects and continuously improve your service. When you spot a pattern - like AI consistently struggling with certain poses or angles - you can develop specific techniques to address these challenges proactively.

Remember, quality control isn't about perfection - it's about delivering consistent, professional results that solve your clients' needs. Build these quality checks into your regular workflow, and they'll become second nature.

### ACTION ITEMS

- ☐ Keep a record of quality issues
- ☐ Develop specific techniques for common issues
- ☐ Implement quality checks throughout your workflow
- ☐ Test your quality control system with a sample project

## SERVICE DESCRIPTION TEMPLATES

Writing a compelling service description requires balancing detail with clarity. Your description needs to tell potential clients exactly what they'll get while building confidence in your expertise. Let's break this down into its essential components.

Start with a clear, benefit-focused headline. Instead of simply stating "AI Image Generation," lead with something like "Professional AI Product Photography: Studio-Quality Images in 3

Days." This immediately tells clients what they'll get and how quickly they'll get it.

In your main description, walk clients through what working with you looks like. Explain that they'll receive ten high-quality product images, each crafted to professional studio standards. Mention specific features like your white background option and multiple angle compositions – these details help clients visualize the end result. Be explicit about including two rounds of revisions; this reassures clients they'll have opportunities to refine the results.

Timing matters enormously to clients, so be specific about your delivery schedule. A three-day turnaround sounds much more professional than "as soon as possible." Break down what happens during those three days: initial generation, review period, and final delivery. This transparency helps build trust and sets realistic expectations.

Include clear technical specifications as well. Tell clients they'll receive high-resolution files suitable for both web and print use. Specify your file formats and explain that they'll get full commercial usage rights. These technical details demonstrate your professional understanding and prevent misunderstandings later.

Finally, consider adding a brief note about your quality assurance process. Mentioning that each image undergoes a thorough quality check for technical and aesthetic standards helps demonstrate your professionalism and attention to detail.

Remember to keep your language professional but approachable. You're not just selling a technical service – you're offering a solution to their business needs.

### ACTION ITEMS

- ☐ Write a compelling service description
- ☐ Include specific technical details
- ☐ Explain your quality assurance process
- ☐ Set realistic delivery expectations

# THE AI SIDE HUSTLE REVOLUTION

With your service fully set up and tested, you're ready for the most exciting step - getting your first paying client.

## Getting Your First Client

The hardest part of starting any service business isn't the setup - it's getting that first paying client. Let's break down exactly how to make this happen.

### WHERE TO FIND CLIENTS TODAY

Finding your first client doesn't require complex marketing strategies - it requires finding one person who needs exactly what you're offering. The key is looking in places where potential clients are already discussing their AI-related challenges.

Online communities are goldmines for finding clients who need AI arbitrage services. Join Facebook groups focused on e-commerce, where store owners frequently discuss their struggles with product photography. You might spot someone posting: "I've been trying to use Midjourney for product shots, but everything looks weird." That's your opportunity to offer help. Similarly, in business owner groups, watch for posts about content creation challenges or complaints about AI-written content sounding robotic - these are perfect openings for content arbitrage services.

Professional networks like LinkedIn often reveal opportunities for research and document processing arbitrage. When someone posts about spending hours analyzing market reports or struggling to extract insights from business documents, they're signaling a need for your expertise. Look for comments like "We tried using ChatGPT to analyze our customer feedback, but we're not sure if we can trust the results."

Industry-specific forums can be particularly valuable. In tech forums, developers might discuss challenges with AI implementation - an opportunity if you're offering chatbot optimization services. In marketing groups, professionals often share their frustrations with generating consistent social media content, opening the door for your content arbitrage services.

Direct outreach can work well when you spot clear needs. If you notice a local business's website using poor-quality product images, or a company blog filled with generic AI-generated content, these are opportunities to demonstrate how your arbitrage services could help them achieve better results.

The key is engaging authentically in these communities. Don't spam - instead, offer genuine advice and insights. When someone describes a problem you can solve, respond with helpful suggestions first. This builds credibility and often leads to natural conversations about your services.

> **ACTION ITEMS**
>
> ☐ Identify 3 online communities for your service type

## WRITING YOUR FIRST PROPOSAL

When you find a potential client, your proposal should be specific and value-focused. Here's a template:

"Hi [Name],

I noticed you're looking for help with [specific need]. I specialize in creating [service type] for businesses like yours.

Here's what I can deliver: [Specific deliverables] [Timeline] [Price]

I'm currently offering a launch special for new clients: [special offer].

Here's an example of my work: [link to sample]

Would you be interested in discussing this further?

Best, [Your name]"

Keep it short, specific, and focused on their needs.

# THE AI SIDE HUSTLE REVOLUTION

### ACTION ITEMS

- ☐ Write your first proposal
- ☐ Include specific deliverables
- ☐ Set realistic delivery expectations
- ☐ Offer a launch special
- ☐ Provide a sample of your work

## SAMPLE CLIENT MESSAGES

When someone responds, be ready with clear answers to common questions. For example:

On Process: "Here's how we'll work together:

1. You'll share your requirements and any reference images
2. I'll create initial versions for your review
3. You'll provide feedback
4. I'll make revisions
5. You'll receive final files ready to use"

On Revisions: "The package includes two rounds of revisions. This means you'll have multiple opportunities to ensure the images are exactly what you need."

On Timing: "Based on my current project schedule, I can deliver your first draft within [X] business days, with final files following [Y] days after your approval. I'll keep you updated on progress throughout the process."

### ACTION ITEMS

- ☐ Prepare answers to common questions

## HANDLING OBJECTIONS

Common objections and how to handle them:

"That's more than I planned to spend." Response: "I understand. While there are cheaper options, my service saves you time and ensures professional quality. Would you like to hear about my starter package?"

"I'm not sure about using AI images." Response: "I understand the concern. The images we create are commercially licensed and professionally polished. Would you like to see some examples of work I've done for other clients?"

"I need it faster." Response: "I can offer rush delivery for an additional fee. When do you need the final images?"

> **ACTION ITEMS**
>
> ☐ Prepare answers to common objections

## CLOSING THE DEAL

Once there's interest, make it easy to say yes:

1. Provide a clear summary of what they'll get
2. Share your simple payment process
3. Set clear next steps
4. Follow up promptly

For example: "Great! To get started, I'll need:

1. Your payment of \$299 (I'll send a PayPal invoice)
2. Your product details and any reference images
3. Your brand guidelines if available

Once I receive these, I'll start work immediately and have your first drafts within 48 hours."

> **ACTION ITEMS**
>
> ☐ Prepare your standard closing email

## MANAGING EXPECTATIONS

Before starting, ensure the client understands:

- Exactly what they'll receive
- When they'll receive it
- The revision process
- What you need from them
- How to provide feedback

This prevents misunderstandings and ensures a smooth first project.

> **ACTION ITEMS**
>
> ☐ Prepare your standard email for client onboarding

Once you've secured your first client, you need a reliable system to deliver outstanding results. Let's build that system step by step.

### Delivery System

Delivering high-quality AI solutions while balancing your day job requires a structured, repeatable process. In this section, we'll outline exactly how to set up your "Delivery System" so you can handle client projects efficiently without compromising on quality—or your personal schedule. You'll learn how to divide tasks into manageable steps, systematically refine outputs, and keep everything organized to meet deadlines stress-free. By establishing a clear, step-by-step approach, you'll ensure every project is delivered with professional consistency, even when time is limited.

## CLIENT INPUT TEMPLATE

Gathering complete project information upfront saves hours of back-and-forth and ensures you can deliver exactly what your client needs. For AI image generation projects, develop a comprehensive but straightforward way to collect project details from your clients.

Start by asking about the product itself. You'll need more than just its name and basic description – understand its key features, unique selling points, and what makes it special in the market. This context helps you generate images that highlight the right aspects and appeal to the right audience.

Understanding your client's target audience shapes every aspect of the image generation process. Ask about their ideal customer, how these images will be used, and what message they want to convey. A product targeting luxury consumers needs a different visual approach than one aimed at budget-conscious shoppers.

Style preferences matter enormously in delivering satisfying results. Have clients describe their desired aesthetic, whether it's modern and minimalist or warm and traditional. Better yet, ask them to share examples of images they like. These reference images provide invaluable guidance for your prompt engineering.

> **ACTION ITEMS**
>
> - ☐ Create a client questionnaire template
> - ☐ List required technical specifications
> - ☐ Write clear style guide questions
> - ☐ Design a reference image guide
> - ☐ Create a project timeline template

## STEP-BY-STEP DELIVERY PROCESS

Delivering professional AI-generated images while working around a day job requires careful planning and efficient use of your evening hours. Here's how to structure your workflow for consistent, high-quality results.

Begin your first evening with thorough preparation. Review all client inputs carefully, ensuring you understand exactly what they need. Plan your approach, considering which prompt styles might work best for their requirements. Create your initial prompts and run some test generations to validate your approach. This foundation-setting phase prevents wasted time later.

Your second evening focuses on bulk generation. Plan to create between 50 and 100 variations – this might sound like a lot, but AI image generation often requires volume to get the perfect results. Apply the creation phase quality checks from our quality control system as you go, helping you identify the most promising candidates early.

The third evening is all about refinement. Take your best candidates from the previous session and generate targeted variations to perfect them. Run each potential final image through a detailed quality check. Select the strongest options and prepare preview versions for your client. This methodical approach ensures you're only showing your best work.

When sharing with clients, be clear and realistic about your delivery timeline. Consider how many evening hours you can consistently dedicate to client work, and build in buffer time for unexpected challenges. If you're working a day job, be upfront that you'll be working during evening hours. Set expectations that match your actual capacity - it's better to promise a longer timeline and deliver early than to rush and compromise quality.

For example, if you know you can dedicate two hours each evening to client work, and a typical project takes you 6-8 hours, you might quote a 4-5 business day timeline. This gives you flexibility to handle revisions and maintains work-life balance while delivering professional results.

Handle revisions systematically when needed. Apply client feedback precisely, generate new variations as required, and maintain your quality standards throughout. Never skip the quality check, even when working with revisions — consistency is key to professional results.

For final delivery, package everything professionally. Include high-resolution files in appropriate formats, clear usage instructions, and suggestions for future services. Request feedback about their experience, as this information proves invaluable for improving your service.

This evening-based workflow lets you maintain your day job while delivering professional results. The key is breaking the work into manageable chunks and maintaining consistent quality checks throughout the process.

### ACTION ITEMS

- ☐ Create your evening work schedule
- ☐ Set up progress tracking system
- ☐ Write your quality control process
- ☐ Create delivery notification templates
- ☐ Plan your backup workflow for emergencies

## REVISION HANDLING

Managing revisions professionally sets your service apart and turns potentially stressful situations into opportunities to demonstrate your expertise. The key lies in creating a structured process that guides clients toward providing actionable feedback while maintaining clear boundaries around your service.

Start by providing clients with a focused feedback form. Rather than asking for general impressions, guide them to be specific about what's working and what needs adjustment. Ask them to identify which elements they want to keep from the current versions — this prevents unnecessary changes to aspects they already like. Have them describe exactly what needs to change, and encourage them to provide reference images when possible.

Set clear boundaries around your revision process from the start. Explain how many revision rounds are included and what constitutes a revision. This prevents scope creep and helps maintain project profitability. When clients understand the revision framework upfront, they tend to provide more thoughtful, consolidated feedback rather than making changes one at a time.

Document every change request and your response to it. This creates a clear record of the project's evolution and helps prevent misunderstandings. It also builds a valuable knowledge base that helps you anticipate and prevent similar issues in future projects.

### ACTION ITEMS

- ☐ Create a revision request form
- ☐ Set up a revision tracking system
- ☐ Write clear revision policy
- ☐ Create revision pricing tiers
- ☐ Build a revision feedback template

#### FEEDBACK COLLECTION

Gathering client feedback systematically after project completion serves multiple purposes. Beyond improving your service, it provides valuable testimonials and helps identify opportunities for additional services.

Create a simple but comprehensive feedback form that clients can complete quickly. Ask about their overall experience with your service, focusing on what worked well and what could be improved. Frame questions to elicit specific, actionable responses rather than vague impressions. For instance, instead of asking if they liked the service, ask what specific aspects of the process made their experience positive.

Pay particular attention to their thoughts about your communication style, delivery timeline, and revision process.

These operational aspects often matter as much as the final deliverables. Understanding how clients perceive your service structure helps you refine your processes for better efficiency and satisfaction.

Include questions about additional services they might need. This not only helps you plan future offerings but often leads to immediate follow-up work. A client happy with their product photos might mention needing regular social media content, opening the door for an ongoing service relationship.

Use the feedback you collect strategically. Positive comments can become testimonials for your marketing materials, while constructive criticism helps you continuously improve your service. Look for patterns in the feedback – if multiple clients mention similar points, they deserve special attention in your service development.

**ACTION ITEMS**

- ☐ Design your feedback survey
- ☐ Create a testimonial request template
- ☐ Set up feedback tracking system
- ☐ Write follow-up email templates
- ☐ Plan your service improvement process

## PAYMENT PROCESSING

A smooth payment process sets the tone for your entire client relationship. Keep your payment system simple but professional, starting with clear pricing discussions upfront. When a client is ready to proceed, send them a professional invoice that details exactly what they're purchasing and when payment is due.

Offer straightforward payment options that work for both you and your clients. PayPal and Stripe are excellent starting choices – they're widely trusted and easy to use. While you might be tempted to offer every payment method available, remember that more options often mean more complexity in managing your finances.

Your payment terms should be crystal clear. State when payment is due, what it covers, and any relevant policies about refunds or additional charges. For instance, you might require full payment before starting work on smaller projects, while larger projects might warrant a 50% deposit with the balance due upon completion.

Always provide proper receipts for your clients' records. Many of your clients will need these for their business expenses, and providing them promptly demonstrates your professionalism. Consider creating a template that includes all necessary information: your business details, payment amount, services rendered, and payment date.

For your first few clients, keep the payment structure as simple as possible – typically a single payment upfront. As you grow and take on larger projects, you can introduce more sophisticated payment structures like milestone payments or retainer arrangements. The key is matching your payment process to your service's complexity and your clients' needs.

### ACTION ITEMS

- ☐ Set up a payment processor account
- ☐ Create professional invoice template
- ☐ Write payment terms document
- ☐ Build payment tracking system
- ☐ Create payment reminder templates

### Chapter Summary

In this chapter, we've provided a comprehensive guide to building your first AI Service Arbitrage business. We've covered everything from choosing your initial service offering to setting up efficient delivery systems and acquiring your first clients. The focus has been on creating a sustainable operation that can grow alongside your primary career.

We've explored how to identify profitable service opportunities, set appropriate pricing that reflects your value, and validate your service offering before making significant investments. The emphasis has been on building systematic approaches to delivery and quality control that ensure consistent results for your clients.

Most importantly, we've provided practical steps for turning your understanding of AI tools into a viable business. From setting up your workspace to handling client communications and managing revisions, you now have a complete framework for starting your AI Service Arbitrage journey.

As you move forward with implementing these strategies, remember that success in this field comes from consistently delivering value while building systems that allow you to scale efficiently. Your next steps are to choose your specific service offering, set up your initial workflows, and begin reaching out to potential clients.

The beauty of AI Service Arbitrage lies in its scalability. Start small, perfect your processes, and grow at a pace that maintains quality. As you gain experience and testimonials, you can gradually expand your services and increase your rates, building a sustainable business around your expertise in AI tools and quality delivery.

> **KEY TAKEAWAYS**
>
> - Choose services where your expertise adds clear value beyond basic AI tool access
> - Price based on the value you provide to clients, not just your costs
> - Build systematic workflows that ensure consistent, high-quality results
> - Start with a minimum viable service and validate it with real clients
> - Focus on solving specific pain points that clients are actively struggling with
> - Implement quality control systems from the beginning
> - Keep your initial service offering focused and well-defined
> - Create clear processes for client communication and delivery
> - Document your workflows to support future scaling
> - Build a foundation that can grow without requiring constant hands-on effort

CHAPTER 6

# Custom GPT Development

In late 2023, OpenAI quietly launched a feature that would change the landscape of AI entrepreneurship: the ability to create custom GPTs. While the media focused on ChatGPT's growing capabilities, savvy entrepreneurs recognized something more significant – the opportunity to build specialized AI tools that solve specific business problems without writing a single line of code.

What makes custom GPT development particularly exciting for side hustlers? Consider these advantages:

1. Minimal Startup Costs: You can start building with just a $20/month ChatGPT Plus subscription
2. No Coding Required: Success comes from understanding business problems, not technical expertise
3. Perfect Side Hustle Format: Development and maintenance can be managed in evening hours
4. Scalable Revenue: Subscription-based pricing creates predictable, growing income
5. Professional Market Focus: Businesses willingly pay for tools that solve specific problems
6. Early Market Advantage: The custom GPT marketplace is still young and growing rapidly

Let's put this opportunity in perspective with a conservative example: Imagine creating a specialized GPT for real estate agents that writes property listings. With just 20 paying customers at $49/month, you're generating $980 in monthly revenue. Keep 70%

after platform fees, and you're looking at $686 monthly income – from a tool that required no coding and minimal startup costs. By month 6, with steady growth and good retention, that could grow to 74 customers generating over $2,500 monthly. And that's just one GPT, serving one specific need, in one industry.

Is this guaranteed? Of course not. But these numbers aren't fantasy either – they represent a realistic scenario based on current market conditions. The key is that custom GPTs allow you to tap into professional markets where users already spend significant time and money solving specific problems. When you can save a real estate agent 30 minutes per listing or help a lawyer draft documents more efficiently, the value proposition becomes crystal clear.

Think of it like being an app developer in the early days of smartphones. Back then, visionary entrepreneurs saw beyond the basic capabilities of mobile devices to imagine specialized apps that would transform how we live and work. Today, we're at a similar inflection point with custom GPTs. While anyone can use ChatGPT's basic features, there's growing demand for specialized AI tools that understand specific industries, speak particular professional languages, and solve unique business challenges.

What makes this opportunity particularly exciting for side hustlers is its accessibility. You don't need a computer science degree or coding expertise to create a successful custom GPT business. Instead, success comes from understanding specific industry needs and crafting focused solutions that deliver real value. Whether it's a specialized tool for real estate agents writing property listings, a legal research assistant that helps lawyers draft case summaries, or a restaurant menu optimization system – the opportunities are as diverse as the business world itself.

In this chapter, you'll learn how to build, launch, and monetize custom GPTs that solve real business problems. We'll walk through everything from identifying profitable opportunities to creating your first GPT, from optimizing its performance to marketing it effectively. By the end, you'll have a complete roadmap for building a sustainable custom GPT business that generates income while you sleep.

But first, let's understand exactly where the money-making opportunities lie in this growing market.

> **ACTION ITEMS**
>
> ☐ Sign up for ChatGPT Plus subscription
> ☐ List 3 industries you know well
> ☐ Identify 5 specific business problems in these industries
> ☐ Research existing AI solutions in your target market
> ☐ Write down your unique value proposition

## Understanding the Market

Before diving into GPT development, let's understand exactly where the money-making opportunities lie. The custom GPT market isn't about building generic AI tools – it's about creating specialized solutions for specific professional needs. Think of it like being a boutique software developer, but without the coding complexity.

Three distinct markets have emerged in the custom GPT landscape, each offering unique opportunities for side hustlers:

### INDUSTRY-SPECIFIC GPTS

These are specialized tools built for particular professional sectors. Our real estate GPT example perfectly illustrates this category – it's not just a writing tool, but a specialized assistant that understands MLS guidelines, property descriptions, and real estate compliance requirements. Similarly, a restaurant menu GPT needs to understand food descriptions, pricing psychology, and local market trends.

The beauty of industry-specific GPTs lies in their focused value proposition. While a restaurant owner might hesitate to pay for a general-purpose AI tool, they'll gladly invest $49/month in a specialized assistant that helps them optimize menu descriptions, pricing, and seasonal specials. With over 660,000 restaurants in the United States alone, capturing even a tiny market share can generate significant recurring revenue.

## TASK-SPECIFIC GPTS

These tools excel at particular business functions across industries. Consider a proposal writing GPT that helps consultants craft winning business proposals, or a social media content GPT that maintains brand voice while generating engaging posts. These tools succeed because they focus on doing one thing exceptionally well.

The market for task-specific GPTs is growing rapidly as businesses look to automate specific workflows without hiring additional staff. A well-designed email response GPT might sell for $29/month to freelancers and small business owners who need professional-quality client communications without spending hours writing emails.

## PROCESS-SPECIFIC GPTS

These GPTs optimize particular business workflows, like employee onboarding, compliance documentation, or financial reporting. They're valuable because they encode best practices into an easy-to-use interface, ensuring consistency while saving time.

A compliance documentation GPT might command $99/month from small law firms or HR departments because it helps them maintain consistent, accurate records while reducing the risk of errors or omissions.

## MARKET RESEARCH PROCESS

Your first week of evening sessions should focus on validating your GPT idea before investing significant development time. Each evening has a specific focus, building on the previous day's insights to create a comprehensive understanding of your market opportunity.

Begin your first evening with market size assessment. This foundational work helps you understand if your idea has enough potential to justify the investment. Pull up your favorite spreadsheet and start with concrete numbers:

For example, if you're considering a real estate listing GPT, research:

- Total number of active real estate agents in your target market
- Average number of listings each agent handles monthly
- Typical time spent writing property descriptions
- Current costs for similar tools or services
- Industry-standard pricing for related software

Don't just collect numbers – analyze what they mean for your business. If there are 100,000 active agents in your market, and 10% might be interested in AI tools, that's 10,000 potential users. If they typically spend 30-45 minutes per listing description and value their time at $100/hour, you can start calculating the potential value your GPT provides.

Document everything systematically:

- Primary market size (total professionals in the field)
- Serviceable market (those likely to use AI tools)
- Target market share (realistic percentage you could capture)
- Competitor pricing ranges
- Your projected pricing and revenue models

This research doesn't need to be perfect, but it needs to be thorough enough to either validate your idea or signal that you should pivot to a different opportunity. The goal isn't to prove your idea will succeed – it's to ensure it has enough potential to justify your time investment.

Remember, successful GPTs often serve surprisingly specific niches. While the total market might be smaller, focused solutions typically command higher prices and face less competition. A GPT that helps luxury real estate agents write compelling descriptions for high-end properties might have a smaller total market than a general-purpose real estate GPT, but could justify premium pricing through specialized expertise.

With your market size validated, spend your second evening analyzing the competition. This isn't just about knowing who else is out there – it's about understanding where opportunities exist for meaningful differentiation. Study both GPT and non-GPT solutions to understand:

- Existing solutions and their limitations
- Current pricing models and feature sets
- Common user complaints
- Unmet needs and wishes
- Your potential competitive advantages

Your third evening focuses on deep user research. This is where many GPT creators rush or skip entirely, but it's crucial for success. Immerse yourself in your target users' world:

- Join industry-specific forums
- Read professional group discussions
- Note recurring problems and frustrations
- Document specific terminology
- List common workflows

Your fourth evening focuses on developing a compelling value proposition. This is where you articulate the benefits of your GPT and how it solves specific professional problems. Consider:

- Calculate time/money saved
- List specific problems solved
- Outline unique features
- Draft pricing scenarios
- Define success metrics

Your fifth evening focuses on validation. This is where you create a simple landing page and gather initial feedback to confirm your pricing assumptions and understand user demand.

Your goal isn't to build the next ChatGPT – it's to create a focused solution that serves a specific market need. Success in the custom

GPT space comes from understanding and solving real professional problems, not from having the most advanced technical features.

For example, if you're building that restaurant menu GPT, your research might reveal that restaurants struggle most with seasonal menu updates and price optimization. This insight helps you focus your development efforts on these high-value features rather than trying to build every possible capability.

Remember, you're not just selling AI technology – you're selling solutions to business problems. Your market research should focus on understanding these problems deeply so you can create a GPT that solves them effectively.

> **ACTION ITEMS**
>
> ☐ Calculate total addressable market size
> ☐ List top 3 competitors and their pricing
> ☐ Join 3 industry-specific communities
> ☐ Document 5 common pain points
> ☐ Identify underserved market segments
> ☐ Test initial pricing assumptions

### Development Process

Creating a successful custom GPT requires a systematic approach that fits within your evening hours. While traditional software development demands complex tools and extensive coding knowledge, custom GPT development is remarkably accessible. Think of it like building a specialized tool – one that needs to be powerful enough to solve real problems while remaining intuitive enough for immediate use.

Your development journey begins with a well-organized workspace. You'll need a ChatGPT Plus subscription ($20/month) and a simple folder structure on your computer. Create a main project folder with clear subfolders: 'knowledge-base' for your core materials, 'prompts' for your interaction templates, 'testing' for validation scenarios, and 'documentation' for user guides and technical notes. This organization becomes crucial as you iterate on your GPT's capabilities.

The foundation of your GPT lies in its knowledge base. For our real estate GPT example, this includes gathering MLS guidelines, property feature descriptions, legal requirements, and brand voice examples. Structure this information in clear categories - core requirements, style guides, and example outputs. A well-organized knowledge base might include a 'listings.md' file with 20-30 high-performing property descriptions, a 'compliance.md' file containing MLS guidelines, and a 'style.md' file documenting preferred terminology and tone.

> **ACTION ITEMS**
>
> - Create your GPT's core system prompt
> - Build a knowledge base folder structure
> - Gather industry-specific guidelines
> - Compile example outputs and templates
> - Test prompt variations
> - Document best-performing approaches

Prompt engineering becomes your primary development tool. Start with a system prompt that defines your GPT's core behavior. For a real estate GPT, this might be:

"You are an expert real estate listing writer with deep knowledge of MLS guidelines and property marketing. Your primary goal is helping real estate agents create compelling, compliant property descriptions. Always maintain a professional tone, emphasize property benefits, and ensure all descriptions meet MLS character limits and compliance requirements."

Build your interaction prompts in layers. Begin with basic input templates:

- Property basics (bedrooms, bathrooms, square footage)
- Special features and upgrades
- Location highlights
- Target buyer profile
- Desired tone and style

Then create output templates that ensure consistent, high-quality results:

- Attention-grabbing headline (under 70 characters)
- Opening hook (2-3 compelling sentences)
- Feature highlights (3-5 bullet points)
- Detailed description (2-3 paragraphs)
- Call to action

For example, a basic input prompt might look like this:

"Create a property listing for a {property_type} with {bedrooms} bedrooms and {bathrooms} bathrooms. Square footage: {sqft}. Key features include {feature_1}, {feature_2}, and {feature_3}. Located in {neighborhood} with {location_benefits}. Target buyers are {buyer_profile}. Tone should be {tone_preference}."

Your GPT should then transform this structured input into compelling output. For instance:

Input:

- Property type: Single-family home
- Bedrooms: 4
- Bathrooms: 2.5
- Square footage: 2,800
- Features: Renovated kitchen, south-facing garden, home office
- Location: Riverside Heights, walking distance to shops and parks
- Target buyers: Young families
- Tone: Sophisticated but welcoming

Output: "Stunning Modern Haven in Coveted Riverside Heights | 4BR/2.5BA Family Sanctuary

Discover refined living in this meticulously updated 2,800 sq ft residence, where modern comfort meets timeless elegance. The chef's kitchen, completely renovated with premium finishes, opens to a sun-drenched family room overlooking a private south-facing garden.

Key Features: • Gourmet kitchen with waterfall quartz counters and professional-grade appliances • Dedicated home office with built-in shelving and natural light • Primary suite with spa-inspired ensuite and walk-in closet • Prime location minutes from boutique shopping and scenic parks

Perfect for discerning families, this turnkey residence offers the ideal balance of sophisticated design and practical living spaces. The flowing floor plan creates natural gathering areas while providing quiet spaces for work and relaxation.

Contact us today to experience the perfect blend of luxury and livability in Riverside Heights."

This structured approach to prompt engineering ensures consistent, high-quality outputs while making it easy to adjust tone, style, and focus based on user preferences. Test your prompts extensively with various inputs to ensure they handle edge cases gracefully while maintaining your desired quality standards.

Quality control must be systematic. Create a testing framework that validates outputs against industry standards:

1. Accuracy Testing

- Compare generated listings with your exemplars
- Verify all property details are correctly represented
- Check compliance with MLS guidelines
- Validate pricing and market claims

2. Consistency Testing

- Run the same inputs multiple times
- Test across different property types

- Verify tone and style consistency
- Check for repetitive phrases or patterns

3. Edge Case Testing

- Unusual property features
- Challenging market conditions
- Complex pricing scenarios
- Special listing requirements

### ACTION ITEMS

- ☐ Set up development workspace
- ☐ Create testing scenarios
- ☐ Build initial prompt library
- ☐ Document edge cases
- ☐ Test with sample inputs
- ☐ Measure response quality
- ☐ Track performance metrics

A typical four-week development timeline might look like this:

Week 1 (Evening Hours): Monday-Tuesday: Set up your workspace and gather core materials Wednesday-Thursday: Build initial knowledge base Friday: Create basic prompt structures

Week 2: Monday-Tuesday: Develop core functionality Wednesday-Thursday: Initial testing and documentation Friday: Begin gathering user feedback

Week 3: Monday-Tuesday: Refine prompts based on feedback Wednesday-Thursday: Expand test scenarios Friday: Quality control improvements

Week 4: Monday-Tuesday: Final functionality polish Wednesday-Thursday: Comprehensive testing Friday: Prepare for launch

Each evening session should last 2-3 hours, maintaining the side hustle time constraint while ensuring professional results. The key is consistent, focused effort rather than marathon sessions.

Remember that development doesn't end at launch. Plan for ongoing optimization based on user feedback and performance metrics. Set up simple systems to track:

- Response accuracy rates
- User satisfaction scores
- Common failure points
- Feature usage patterns
- Performance bottlenecks

Throughout this process, maintain laser focus on your target users' needs. It's easy to get caught up in technical capabilities and forget that success comes from solving real problems effectively. Every development decision should tie back to delivering value for your specific market.

### Store Listing & Monetization

The journey from a well-crafted GPT to a profitable business hinges on how you position and monetize your creation. Think of your GPT store listing as your digital storefront – it needs to do more than just list features. It needs to tell a compelling story about how you solve real problems for your target users.

Your store listing is often your only chance to make a first impression. While technical capabilities matter, what really drives conversions is your ability to connect with your audience's daily challenges. For instance, instead of promoting your real estate GPT as an "AI-powered description generator," position it as "Your 24/7 listing partner: Create MLS-compliant property descriptions in under 5 minutes." This immediate focus on outcomes helps potential customers envision the value in their own work context.

When structuring your pricing strategy, think in terms of value delivered rather than features provided. Consider the real estate agent who typically spends 30-45 minutes crafting each property description. If your GPT helps them create better descriptions in 5 minutes, that's a clear ROI proposition. A $49 monthly subscription becomes an easy decision when it saves hours of valuable time each month.

Start with a tiered pricing approach that creates natural upgrade paths:

A free tier serves as your market entry point, letting users experience your GPT's core value while maintaining clear limitations. Maybe they can generate three listings per month – enough to prove your value but not enough to eliminate the need for a paid plan.

Your professional tier, priced between $29-99 monthly depending on your market, should remove meaningful friction from your users' workflows. This might include higher usage limits, priority processing, or advanced features like brand voice customization.

For enterprise users, consider custom packages that might include dedicated support, team collaboration features, or integration capabilities. While this tier might seem beyond the scope of a side hustle, having it available signals professionalism and creates room for growth.

Usage limits require careful consideration. While it's tempting to be generous, remember that each interaction has associated costs. Structure your limits to ensure profitability while meeting realistic usage patterns. A real estate agent might need 20-30 listings per month, while a restaurant owner updating their menu might only need 5-10 detailed item descriptions.

Monitor your metrics religiously from day one. Key performance indicators should include:

- Conversion rate from free to paid users (aim for 2-3%)
- Average revenue per user (track by tier)
- Usage patterns (peak times, common features)
- Customer lifetime value
- Support ticket frequency

For example, with 1,000 monthly store visitors and a 2% conversion rate to your $49 professional tier, you could generate $686 monthly after platform fees. This conservative projection provides a baseline for measuring success and planning improvements.

Let's break down a realistic revenue model for a professional-tier GPT:

Monthly Visitors: 1,000 Free Trial Users (10% of visitors): 100 Conversion to Paid (2% of visitors): 20 new customers Monthly Price: $49 Gross Monthly Revenue: $980 Platform Fees (30%): $294 Net Monthly Revenue: $686

Factor in customer retention rates – if you maintain an 80% monthly retention rate, by month 6 you could have:

- Month 1: 20 customers ($686 net)
- Month 2: 36 customers ($1,235 net)
- Month 3: 49 customers ($1,680 net)
- Month 4: 59 customers ($2,023 net)
- Month 5: 67 customers ($2,297 net)
- Month 6: 74 customers ($2,537 net)

These numbers assume consistent marketing efforts and product quality. While actual results will vary, this model demonstrates how a focused GPT business can generate meaningful side income through steady growth and strong retention.

Remember that your pricing and positioning strategy isn't set in stone. Start conservative and adjust based on market feedback. It's easier to lower prices than raise them, and easier to add features than remove them. Most importantly, ensure every aspect of your listing and pricing strategy aligns with your target users' needs and expectations.

The key to successful monetization isn't maximizing short-term revenue – it's creating sustainable value that keeps users engaged and willing to pay month after month. Focus on solving real problems effectively, and the revenue will follow naturally.

> **ACTION ITEMS**
>
> ☐ Write compelling store description
> ☐ Create tiered pricing structure
> ☐ Set up payment processing
> ☐ Define usage limits
> ☐ Create onboarding materials
> ☐ Plan upgrade paths
> ☐ Track key performance metrics

## Marketing Your GPT

Marketing a custom GPT requires a different approach than traditional software promotion. Your potential users aren't just looking for tools – they're searching for solutions to specific professional challenges. Success comes from positioning your GPT as the expert solution they've been seeking.

Store optimization forms your marketing foundation. Think of the GPT store like a specialized app store where professionals go to find tools that make their work easier. Your GPT's visibility depends heavily on how well you optimize your listing for both search and conversion. Beyond the basics we covered in the store listing section, focus on creating a compelling narrative that resonates with your target users' daily challenges.

For instance, if you've built a GPT for real estate agents, your marketing should speak directly to their pain points: "Stop spending hours crafting property descriptions. Create engaging, MLS-compliant listings in minutes." This direct connection between their problem and your solution drives both discovery and adoption.

Off-platform promotion amplifies your reach significantly. Professional communities, industry forums, and social media platforms where your target users gather become valuable marketing channels. But remember – you're not just promoting a tool, you're sharing a solution. Create content that demonstrates your GPT solving real problems in your target industry.

Demo videos become particularly powerful here. Show your GPT in action, handling real-world scenarios that your target users face daily. Keep these videos focused and brief – professionals want to see exactly how your tool will save them time or improve their work. A three-minute video showing how your real estate GPT transforms basic property details into compelling listings will likely convert better than a longer, feature-focused presentation.

Building social proof requires a systematic approach. Start with beta users from your target industry, gather their feedback and testimonials, and showcase their success stories. These early adopters often become your most valuable marketing assets, especially when they share their experiences within their professional networks.

Professional communities offer unique marketing opportunities, but they require a thoughtful approach. Instead of direct promotion, focus on being helpful. Share insights about industry challenges, offer solutions (some of which might involve your GPT), and establish yourself as a knowledgeable resource. This builds trust and creates organic interest in your tool.

Cross-promotion strategies work particularly well in the GPT ecosystem. If you've built multiple GPTs serving different aspects of the same industry, each one can help market the others. A real estate agent using your listing description GPT might also be interested in your property analysis GPT or your real estate email marketing assistant.

Remember that marketing a GPT is an ongoing process, not a one-time effort. Monitor your analytics to understand which marketing channels drive the most valuable users. Pay attention to user feedback and incorporate it into both your marketing messages and your GPT's functionality. Success often comes from this continuous loop of feedback and improvement.

The most effective marketing often comes from your existing users. Make it easy for satisfied customers to share their success stories. Consider creating case studies that showcase specific results:

"How Agent Jane Smith increased her listing views by 40% using Real Estate Listing Pro GPT." These concrete examples help potential users understand the real-world value of your tool.

As your user base grows, consider building a community around your GPT. This might start as a simple feedback channel but can evolve into a valuable resource where users share tips, success stories, and best practices. Such communities often become powerful marketing engines, attracting new users through word-of-mouth and demonstrated success.

The next section will explore how to build effective user support systems that keep your customers happy and your business growing sustainably. After all, the best marketing comes from satisfied users who eagerly recommend your GPT to their colleagues.

### ACTION ITEMS

- ☐ Optimize store listing for discovery
- ☐ Create demonstration videos
- ☐ Build social proof collection system
- ☐ Join professional communities
- ☐ Plan content marketing calendar
- ☐ Set up analytics tracking
- ☐ Monitor user engagement metrics

### User Support Systems

Supporting users of your custom GPT requires a different mindset than traditional software support. Your users aren't just learning to use a tool – they're integrating AI into their professional workflows. This transition often requires both technical guidance and strategic support to help them achieve their desired outcomes.

Start by establishing clear support channels that match your users' preferences. While email support might work well for some professional audiences, others might prefer instant messaging or community forums. The key is making support accessible without creating an overwhelming maintenance burden for you as a side hustler.

Documentation forms the foundation of your support system. Create clear, action-oriented guides that walk users through common workflows. Instead of generic feature descriptions, focus on specific use cases. For instance, a real estate GPT's documentation might include step-by-step guides for "Creating Your First Property Listing" or "Optimizing Listings for Different Platforms."

FAQ development should be proactive rather than reactive. Anticipate common questions by documenting the issues you encountered during testing. Pay particular attention to edge cases and limitations – users appreciate honesty about what your GPT can and cannot do. Update your FAQs regularly based on actual user questions, creating a living resource that grows more valuable over time.

When handling support issues, look for patterns that suggest opportunities for improvement. If multiple users struggle with a particular feature, that's a signal to either enhance the functionality or improve its documentation. Remember, every support interaction is a chance to learn about your users' needs and refine your product.

Update communications deserve special attention. When you enhance your GPT or add new features, communicate these changes effectively. Don't just list technical updates – explain how these improvements help users achieve their goals. "We've enhanced our property description algorithm to better highlight unique features" is more meaningful than "Updated description generation system."

Feedback collection should be systematic but unobtrusive. Create simple ways for users to share their experiences and suggestions. This might be through brief surveys, feedback forms, or community discussions. The goal is gathering insights that help you improve your GPT while respecting your users' time.

Community building becomes particularly valuable as your user base grows. A well-managed community can become a powerful support resource, where experienced users help newcomers and share best practices. Start small – perhaps with a simple discussion forum or social media group – and let it grow organically based on user engagement.

Remember that support isn't just about solving problems – it's about helping users succeed. When users share their challenges, look beyond the immediate issue to understand their underlying goals. Often, you can suggest alternative approaches or features they might not have considered, turning support interactions into opportunities for user education and engagement.

As your side hustle grows, consider creating templates and systems that help you provide consistent, efficient support without consuming too much of your time. Document common responses, create troubleshooting flowcharts, and develop clear escalation procedures for complex issues. The goal is maintaining high-quality support while preserving the time-leveraged nature of your business.

The most successful custom GPT businesses often distinguish themselves through superior support. While competitors might offer similar technical capabilities, your understanding of user needs and commitment to their success can create lasting competitive advantages. This approach not only reduces churn but also generates valuable word-of-mouth marketing from satisfied users.

### ACTION ITEMS

- ☐ Create support documentation
- ☐ Set up feedback channels
- ☐ Build FAQ database
- ☐ Create response templates
- ☐ Document common issues
- ☐ Plan support workflow
- ☐ Establish response time goals

## Growth & Scaling

Growing a custom GPT business requires a delicate balance between expansion and sustainability. Unlike traditional software businesses that often chase rapid growth at any cost, your side hustle needs to scale in a way that preserves its part-time nature while increasing revenue and impact.

Analytics form the foundation of intelligent growth. Beyond basic usage metrics, pay attention to patterns that reveal opportunities. Which features do your most successful users rely on most heavily? What time of day do they typically use your GPT? Understanding these patterns helps you make informed decisions about where to focus your development efforts.

Version updates should follow a clear strategy. Rather than adding features simply because you can, focus on improvements that directly impact user success. When your analytics show that users consistently struggle with a particular task, or frequently request a specific capability, you've found your next development priority. This targeted approach ensures your time investment delivers maximum value.

Feature expansion works best when it follows natural usage patterns. For instance, if your real estate listing GPT is successful, users might naturally want help with property analysis or market comparisons. These adjacent capabilities create natural growth opportunities without straying from your core value proposition. The key is expanding in ways that complement rather than complicate your existing offering.

User feedback becomes increasingly valuable as you scale. Create systematic ways to gather and analyze user insights. This might include quarterly surveys, user interviews, or analysis of support tickets. Look for patterns that suggest new opportunities or reveal hidden pain points. The goal isn't just to fix problems but to identify opportunities for meaningful growth.

Portfolio development requires strategic thinking. As you consider adding new GPTs to your lineup, look for offerings that complement your existing products. A real estate agent using your listing GPT might also need help with market analysis reports, client communications, or social media marketing. Each new addition should leverage your existing knowledge while serving a distinct need.

Cross-selling opportunities emerge naturally as your portfolio grows. Users who succeed with one of your GPTs become prime candidates for related tools. But remember – the goal isn't to sell more products, it's to solve more problems. Focus on helping users achieve their goals, and sales will follow naturally.

Partnership strategies can accelerate growth without demanding more of your time. Consider collaborating with complementary service providers, industry influencers, or professional associations. These relationships can bring new users to your GPTs while providing additional value to your existing customers.

As you scale, maintain your focus on solving specific problems exceptionally well. It's better to be the go-to solution for a particular need than to offer mediocre solutions for many problems. This focused approach not only makes your GPTs more valuable but also keeps your business manageable as a side hustle.

Remember that sustainable growth often comes from deepening relationships with existing users rather than constantly chasing new ones. When users find genuine value in your GPT, they become advocates who bring others to your solution. This organic growth typically proves more sustainable than aggressive marketing campaigns.

The most successful GPT businesses grow through a combination of product excellence and user advocacy. By maintaining high standards while expanding thoughtfully, you create a virtuous cycle where satisfied users drive growth through recommendations and testimonials.

> **ACTION ITEMS**
>
> - ☐ Track key growth metrics
> - ☐ Plan feature roadmap
> - ☐ Document scaling triggers
> - ☐ Create expansion strategy
> - ☐ Build referral system
> - ☐ Monitor user satisfaction
> - ☐ Plan resource allocation

## Chapter Summary

Throughout this chapter, we've explored the complete journey of building a successful custom GPT business as a side hustle. From identifying market opportunities to scaling your business, we've seen how accessible yet powerful this business model can be for entrepreneurs willing to focus on solving specific problems well.

The key to success in the custom GPT market isn't technical complexity – it's understanding and serving specific professional needs. Whether you're creating tools for real estate agents, legal professionals, or restaurant owners, your success will come from deeply understanding their challenges and crafting focused solutions that deliver real value.

We've seen how the development process, while technical in nature, remains accessible to non-programmers. Success comes from systematic approaches to knowledge base building, prompt engineering, and quality control. More importantly, we've learned how to manage this development process within the time constraints of a side hustle, focusing on iterative improvements that consistently add value for users.

Marketing and monetization require thoughtful strategies that align with your users' professional contexts. Rather than aggressive growth tactics, success comes from building trust, demonstrating concrete value, and letting satisfied users become your advocates.

The pricing and positioning strategies we've explored help you capture fair value while keeping your offering accessible to your target market.

User support and scaling strategies complete the picture, showing how to grow your business sustainably without letting it consume your life. By focusing on systematic approaches to support and thoughtful expansion of your offerings, you can build a thriving business that generates significant income while maintaining its part-time nature.

As you move forward with your custom GPT business, remember that success comes from focus rather than breadth. Start with one specific problem for one specific audience, solve it exceptionally well, and let your business grow organically from that strong foundation. The opportunities in this market are vast, but they're best captured through patient, systematic execution rather than trying to do everything at once.

In the next chapter, we'll explore how to build AI-powered content systems, another exciting opportunity in the AI side hustle landscape. You'll see how the principles we've discussed here – focusing on specific needs, building systematic solutions, and scaling thoughtfully – apply equally well in different contexts.

### KEY TAKEAWAYS

- Focus on solving specific professional problems rather than building generic AI tools
- Success comes from understanding industry needs, not technical complexity
- Build a comprehensive knowledge base before starting development
- Create systematic approaches to prompt engineering and quality control
- Start with a minimum viable GPT and iterate based on user feedback
- Price based on the value you deliver to professionals, not your development costs
- Implement user support systems that scale with your business
- Document everything for future improvements and scaling
- Focus on one industry or problem space initially
- Build for sustainable growth that fits your side hustle schedule

CHAPTER 7

# AI-Powered Content Systems

Imagine waking up to find that while you slept, your AI content systems generated three new books, published fifteen blog posts, created twenty social media updates, and most importantly - made money. This isn't science fiction. The tools exist today to build automated content systems that work while you sleep.

Welcome to the world of AI-powered content systems - where you build once and profit repeatedly.

The opportunity is unique: AI tools can now generate quality content at scale, automation can handle distribution, and platforms are hungry for consistent content. But the real magic isn't in using AI to write content - it's in building systems that create, distribute, and monetize content automatically.

In this chapter, you'll learn how to build these systems. We'll explore exciting possibilities from book publishing engines to digital asset factories. You'll get a clear roadmap for building your own content system, with step-by-step guidance for your first week and month. Most importantly, you'll see how to create something that can generate value for years to come.

## Understanding Content Systems

At their core, AI content systems are about automation and scalability. They take your initial setup and guidance, then multiply your efforts through intelligent workflows. A well-built system handles everything from content creation to distribution to monetization - with minimal ongoing oversight.

Think of your content system like a smart factory. Raw materials (ideas, data, or prompts) enter one end, and polished, profitable content emerges from the other. The key isn't just using AI tools - it's building processes that maintain quality and consistency at scale.

The most successful content systems share three core elements working together in harmony. At their heart lies intelligent content generation that maintains both quality and variety, ensuring fresh material that meets consistent standards. This works alongside automated distribution systems that ensure content reaches the right audiences at the right time. Finally, smart monetization ties everything together, creating sustainable revenue streams that grow over time. When these elements work in concert, they create a truly automated content engine.

### ACTION ITEMS

- ☐ Choose one primary content type to focus on
- ☐ List 3 repetitive tasks in your workflow
- ☐ Identify your target audience
- ☐ Research top AI tools for your content type
- ☐ Set clear quality standards
- ☐ Define your success metrics

## Content System Possibilities

The world of AI-Powered content systems offers a vast landscape of opportunities. Let's explore some exciting possibilities that could spark your creativity and show you what's achievable with the right system.

### DIGITAL ASSET FACTORY

Imagine a design system that works while you sleep, generating dozens of new variations from a single template. Your initial creation

# THE AI SIDE HUSTLE REVOLUTION

- perhaps a pitch deck or social media kit - could automatically spawn into different color schemes, alternative layouts, and seasonal versions. Think beyond basic slides: your system could produce UX wireframes adapting to various devices, social media templates matching emerging trends, or email designs scaling across industries.

The real magic happens in specialized niches. Picture scientific poster templates automatically following different journal guidelines, or educational worksheets generating infinite practice variations. Every professional field needs well-designed assets - your system could serve these specific needs at scale.

## YOUTUBE CONTENT FACTORY

Envision a content engine transforming raw data into compelling visual stories. Your system could turn market trends into dynamic charts, historical events into animated timelines, or complex concepts into clear explanations. Each video might automatically generate its own thumbnails, descriptions, and tags, building a growing library of valuable content.

The possibilities extend far beyond basic facts. Imagine channels exploring historical mysteries, breaking down scientific discoveries, or explaining emerging technologies - all through automated research, scripting, and visualization. Your system could even adapt content for different audience levels, creating multiple versions of each explanation.

## PODCAST EMPIRE

Consider building a podcast factory that never sleeps. Your system could research topics, write scripts, generate natural-sounding voices, and publish episodes automatically. Picture running multiple shows simultaneously: daily news summaries, educational series, storytelling channels - each with its own voice and style, but all powered by your core system.

The exciting part? Your podcast factory could extend beyond audio. Each episode might automatically generate its own show notes, social media posts, and promotional materials. You'd be building a content ecosystem, not just individual shows.

## BOOK PUBLISHING ENGINE

Imagine a book creation system handling everything from concept to publication. In fiction, your system could generate engaging stories across multiple genres, each following proven storytelling patterns while maintaining unique voices. For non-fiction, think about creating educational guides, how-to manuals, or expert handbooks - all systematically researched, written, and formatted.

The potential grows with automation. Your system could manage multiple pen names, each with its own style and genre focus. It might handle everything from cover design to blurb writing, from formatting to publishing, creating a truly hands-off book production line.

## EDUCATIONAL CONTENT NETWORK

Picture a learning system that never runs out of material. Your automation could generate unlimited math problems with step-by-step solutions, language learning exercises adapting to student levels, or coding challenges with automatic testing. Think about creating content serving different learning styles: visual guides, practice exercises, quick references, and comprehensive explanations.

The real power comes from interconnection. Your system could link concepts, build progressive learning paths, and create supporting materials automatically. Imagine building a knowledge network that grows and improves itself over time.

## LOCAL GUIDE SYSTEMS

Envision a hyperlocal content engine that knows your city inside and out. Your system could discover hidden gems, track upcoming events, and generate neighborhood guides automatically. Consider building themed exploration guides: foodie tours, historical walks, family activities - each automatically updated with fresh content and seasonal relevance.

The beauty of local content? Every city needs it, and you could start with just one neighborhood, perfecting your system before expanding to other areas.

## SOCIAL MEDIA NETWORKS

Imagine orchestrating a network of content channels working together seamlessly. Your system could adapt content for each platform's unique requirements, generate engaging visuals, and maintain consistent posting schedules across multiple accounts. Think about building theme-based networks: inspiration quotes, industry insights, trend analysis - each feeding into a larger content ecosystem.

The possibilities are truly endless. Whether you choose to focus on one content type or combine several approaches, the opportunity lies in creating systems that generate value automatically. The key is to start with one area that aligns with your interests and skills, then build from there.

Now that we've explored the exciting landscape of content systems, let's dive into how you can start building your own...

### ACTION ITEMS

- ☐ Pick one content system type to start with
- ☐ List your relevant skills and experience
- ☐ Research required tools and costs
- ☐ Find 3 successful examples in your chosen area
- ☐ Identify your unique angle or niche
- ☐ Write down your 30-day goal

## Your First Steps

Embarking on your content system journey is exciting, but it's important to move at a pace that works for you. Everyone's path will be different, depending on their chosen system, prior experience, and available time. Here are the key first steps to take, in an order that makes sense for most beginners:

1. Choose Your System Start by selecting the content type that aligns with your skills and interests. Whether it's a digital asset factory, a book publishing engine, or an educational content network, your choice will guide all future steps.

2. Learn Your Tools Familiarize yourself with the AI and creation tools central to your system. This might mean exploring AI writing assistants, image generators, or voice synthesis tools. Take the time to understand their capabilities and limitations.

3. Create Test Content Before diving into automation, generate some test content manually. This hands-on experience is crucial for understanding your system's needs and challenges. Create a small batch of whatever your system will produce: a few digital assets, a short ebook, or a set of educational materials.

4. Design Your Workflow Map out the steps your content will go through, from initial idea to final publication. Think about how you'll maintain quality and consistency as you scale. This workflow will be the blueprint for your future automation.

5. Explore Basic Automation Once you're comfortable with manual creation, start investigating tools that can automate parts of your workflow. This might be as simple as scheduling social media posts or as complex as setting up AI-powered content generation pipelines. Remember, automation is a gradual process - start small and expand.

6. Publish Your First Piece Get something out into the world. It doesn't need to be perfect, but it should complete the full cycle

from idea to published content. This real-world experience will teach you more than any amount of planning.

7. Reflect and Adjust After your first publication, take time to reflect on what worked well and what needs improvement. Use these insights to refine your workflow and plan your next steps.

Remember, there's no set timeline for these steps. Some might take you a day, others a week or more. The key is consistent progress, learning from each step, and gradually building your system.

---

**ACTION ITEMS**

- ☐ Set up your AI tool accounts
- ☐ Create a basic folder structure
- ☐ Make one piece of test content manually
- ☐ Document each step in your process
- ☐ List tasks that could be automated
- ☐ Test one simple automation
- ☐ Get feedback on your first output

---

Now, let's dive deeper into how to build each component of your content engine…

## Building Your Content Engine

At the heart of every successful content system lies a well-designed content engine - the core machinery that transforms ideas into polished, publishable content. Think of it like building a smart factory: you need the right components working together seamlessly to produce consistent, high-quality output.

Let's explore the essential components that make up your content engine, starting with the foundation: your AI content pipeline. This isn't just about throwing prompts at ChatGPT - it's about creating intelligent workflows that maintain quality and consistency at scale.

The most effective content engines use a series of specialized prompts working together, each handling a specific part of the creation process.

For a book publishing system, your pipeline might start with a prompt that generates creative plot concepts, followed by another that expands these into detailed outlines, and a third that transforms outlines into engaging chapters. A digital asset factory might use one prompt to generate design concepts, another for color variations, and a third for platform-specific adaptations.

The secret to a reliable content pipeline lies in your prompt systems. Think of prompts as recipes - they need precise ingredients and clear instructions to produce consistent results. Successful content creators build prompt libraries, organizing their best-performing prompts for different content types and purposes. They create prompt chains where the output of one prompt becomes the input for another, building increasingly refined content.

But great content isn't just about generation - it's about variation and voice. Your engine needs mechanisms to avoid repetition while maintaining quality. Educational content creators might generate multiple explanations of the same concept, each targeting different learning styles. Book publishers might use prompt variations to maintain consistent character voices across chapters. The goal is controlled creativity - enough variation to keep content fresh, but enough consistency to maintain quality.

Quality assurance forms another crucial component. Rather than checking every piece manually, smart content engines build in automated quality controls. This might mean using AI to check for consistency, scanning for common errors, or flagging potential issues for human review. The key is creating systems that catch problems early, before content moves further down your pipeline.

Finally, your content engine needs robust storage and organization systems. As your content library grows, you'll need clear ways to track what's been created, what's ready for distribution, and what needs revision. Think beyond basic folders

- consider using metadata to track content status, performance metrics, and publication history.

The most sophisticated content engines also include feedback loops. They track which content performs best and automatically adjust generation parameters. A YouTube content factory might notice that videos with certain structures get more engagement, then adapt its prompt systems accordingly. This creates a self-improving engine that gets better over time.

> **ACTION ITEMS**
>
> ☐ Write your core prompt templates
> ☐ Set up your quality control process
> ☐ Create your content organization system
> ☐ Build basic feedback tracking
> ☐ Test your pipeline with sample content
> ☐ Document your workflow steps

Now that we understand the components of our content engine, let's explore how to automate these processes...

## Automation Fundamentals (500 words)

### UNDERSTANDING AUTOMATION THINKING

The journey to building powerful content systems begins with a fundamental shift in how you think about work. Most of us are trained to think in manual, step-by-step processes: write the content, format it, publish it, share it. Automation thinking flips this model on its head. Instead of doing the work, you design systems that do the work for you.

Imagine standing in front of a complex machine in a factory. Your job isn't to operate the machine - it's to design how the machine works. You need to understand the inputs, the processes, and the desired outputs. You need to plan for errors and build in quality checks. This is automation thinking, and it's the key to building successful content systems.

The first step in automation thinking is learning to spot opportunities. Look for any task you do repeatedly. Each time you catch yourself thinking "I need to remember to do this" or "I always have to do that next," you've found an automation opportunity. These moments are gold - they're telling you exactly where your system needs attention.

But here's where many people get stuck: they try to automate everything at once. The secret is thinking in building blocks. Each automation is like a LEGO piece that can connect to others. Start with one block - maybe it's just automatically saving AI-generated content to the right folder. Add another block - perhaps automatic formatting. Then another - maybe quality checking. Soon you have a chain of blocks working together seamlessly.

The real power emerges when you start connecting different tools. Your AI writing assistant might connect to your formatting tool, which connects to your publishing platform, which triggers your social media scheduler. Each connection multiplies the power of your system. This is why successful content creators spend more time planning these connections than actually building them.

Think of yourself as a system designer rather than a content creator. Your job is to:

- Spot repetitive tasks that could be automated
- Design workflows that maintain quality
- Plan how different tools can work together
- Build in monitoring and error handling
- Create systems that can grow over time

This mindset shift takes practice. Start by observing your current content creation process. Where do you spend most of your time? What tasks do you repeat? What steps require your judgment, and what steps are purely mechanical? These observations become the blueprint for your automation journey.

Remember: the goal isn't to automate everything immediately. It's to build sustainable systems that grow with you. Start small, think in blocks, and always plan for connection and expansion. Your future self will thank you for the systems you design today.

> **ACTION ITEMS**
>
> ☐ List all repetitive tasks in your workflow
> ☐ Identify your most time-consuming tasks
> ☐ Map out your basic process flow
> ☐ Choose one task to automate first
> ☐ Research tools for your chosen task
> ☐ Plan your first automation test

Let's look at the core tools that will help you bring these automation ideas to life...

## CORE AUTOMATION TOOLS

The modern automation landscape offers an incredible array of tools, each serving different needs in your content system. Understanding these tools - and more importantly, when to use each one - is crucial for building efficient systems.

Integration platforms form the backbone of most content automation systems. Think of them as digital switchboards, connecting different services and making them work together. Zapier is the perfect starting point - its visual interface lets you create automations by simply connecting triggers ("when this happens") with actions ("do this"). Make.com offers more sophisticated options when you're ready for complex workflows, with better handling of data transformations and multi-step processes.

Several social media platforms offer robust automation capabilities. Buffer and Hootsuite can schedule posts across multiple platforms, automatically reformat content for different networks, and provide analytics that can trigger other automations. Later specializes in visual content scheduling and can automatically post to Instagram, Pinterest, and other image-focused platforms.

Content management systems like WordPress, when combined with plugins like WP Webhooks or AutomatorWP, can trigger actions based on new posts, comments, or user activities. These can connect to your broader automation workflows, making your website an active participant in your content system.

AI tools add another layer of automation possibility. Modern AI services can generate content variations, assist with quality checking, and help maintain consistency across your content. When connected to your automation workflows through APIs, they can process content without human intervention, though you'll want to maintain quality oversight.

The real power emerges when you connect these tools together. An automation might start with AI-generated content, flow through quality checks, move into your scheduling system, and finally publish across multiple platforms - all while notifying you at critical decision points.

Start simple. Build your first automation using just one or two tools. Learn their capabilities and limitations. As your needs grow, gradually incorporate more sophisticated tools and connections. The goal is to create reliable, maintainable systems - not to use every tool available.

### ACTION ITEMS

- ☐ Sign up for one integration platform
- ☐ Connect your primary content tools
- ☐ Set up basic error notifications
- ☐ Create a simple test workflow
- ☐ Document your tool connections
- ☐ Plan your backup procedures

Let's explore the fundamental patterns these tools enable in your automation workflows…

## BASIC AUTOMATION PATTERNS

Think of automation patterns as reliable recipes for your content system. Just as chefs combine basic cooking techniques to create complex dishes, you'll combine these fundamental patterns to build sophisticated content workflows.

### The Trigger-Action-Result Pattern

This is the foundation of all content automation. When something specific happens (trigger), your system performs a defined task (action) to produce a desired outcome (result).

Here's a real example using common tools: When you save a new AI-generated article to a specific Google Drive folder (trigger), Zapier notices the new file and springs into action. It automatically formats the text according to your style guide, adds your standard header image, and inserts your SEO metadata (actions). Finally, it creates a draft post in WordPress ready for your final review (result).

This pattern is incredibly versatile across content types:

- For podcasts: New audio file appears □ Generate show notes □ Create scheduled posts
- For digital assets: New design template uploads □ Create preview images □ List on multiple marketplaces
- For educational content: New lesson outline saves □ Generate practice exercises □ Format for learning platform

The beauty of this pattern is its simplicity and reliability. Each step is clear and trackable, making it easy to troubleshoot when needed.

### The Monitor-Alert-Respond Pattern

The Monitor-Alert-Respond pattern acts like a vigilant assistant for your content system, continuously watching for specific conditions and taking appropriate action. It's particularly powerful for maintaining quality and spotting opportunities.

Here's a practical example: Make (formerly Integromat) monitors your YouTube channel's performance metrics. When viewer retention drops below 40% on new videos (monitor), it sends you a Slack notification with the specific timestamps where viewers are dropping off (alert). It then automatically generates three alternative thumbnail options and title variations for testing (respond).

This pattern shines in various content scenarios:

- For blog networks: Watch traffic patterns □ Alert on engagement drops □ Generate content improvement suggestions
- For digital assets: Track marketplace rankings □ Flag when listings fall below page one □ Automatically refresh keywords and descriptions
- For book publishing: Monitor review sentiment □ Alert on negative patterns □ Generate revision recommendations for future editions

The real power comes from setting up multiple monitoring points. Your system can simultaneously watch content performance, audience engagement, revenue metrics, and competitive positions - each with its own alert thresholds and response actions.

**Create-Transform-Distribute**

This is the workhorse pattern of content systems, turning a single piece of content into multiple assets across different platforms. Think of it as your content multiplication engine.

Here's how it works in practice: Your AI writing tool generates a comprehensive blog post about investment strategies (create). Zapier then triggers a chain of transformations - the post becomes a Twitter thread, a LinkedIn article, and a script for a YouTube video (transform). Finally, Buffer schedules these variations to post across your platforms at optimal times for each audience (distribute).

The pattern becomes even more powerful with specific content types:

- For educational content: Generate detailed lesson □ Create quick-reference guide, practice worksheets, and visual summary □ Distribute across teaching platforms
- For digital assets: Design primary template □ Generate multiple color schemes, size variations, and format options □ List on relevant marketplaces
- For local guides: Write core review □ Transform into map listing, photo gallery, and quick tips □ Share across local platforms and social media

The key to success with this pattern is maintaining quality through each transformation. Your system should preserve the core value of your content while optimizing for each platform's unique requirements. Tools like Make can help by including quality checks between transformations, ensuring each version meets your standards before distribution.

### Combining Patterns for Powerful Workflows

The real magic happens when you combine these patterns into sophisticated workflows. Think of it like building with LEGO - each pattern is a building block that connects with others to create something more powerful.

Here's a real-world example from a content creator's system: The Trigger-Action-Result pattern starts the process when a new AI-generated video script lands in Google Drive. This triggers the Create-Transform-Distribute pattern, which generates the video, social media snippets, and blog post version. Meanwhile, the Monitor-Alert-Respond pattern watches the content's performance across platforms, automatically adjusting posting times and content formats based on engagement data.

These combined patterns create powerful content flows:

- For book publishing: New chapter completion triggers quality checks, generates marketing copy, and monitors early reader feedback to guide revisions
- For digital assets: Template creation spawns variations, distributes to marketplaces, and monitors sales patterns to suggest new design directions
- For educational content: Lesson creation automatically generates supporting materials, tracks student engagement, and adapts difficulty levels based on performance data

The key is starting simple and building up. Begin with one pattern that solves your most pressing need. Once that's running smoothly, add another pattern that enhances its effectiveness. Your system grows more sophisticated while remaining reliable and manageable.

**Starting Your Pattern Journey**

Now that you understand these fundamental patterns, you're ready to implement them in your own content system. The key is choosing the right pattern to solve your most pressing content challenge.

If you're spending hours manually formatting and publishing content, start with Trigger-Action-Result. If you're struggling to keep track of content performance, implement Monitor-Alert-Respond. And if you need to reach audiences across multiple platforms, begin with Create-Transform-Distribute.

Remember: successful automation isn't about building everything at once. Choose one pattern, implement it well, and let it run for a while. Watch how it performs, adjust as needed, and then consider adding more complexity. Your goal is to build a reliable system that grows with you.

> **ACTION ITEMS**
>
> ☐ Choose one automation pattern to start
> ☐ Map out your trigger points
> ☐ List desired actions and results
> ☐ Test pattern with sample content
> ☐ Monitor for potential issues
> ☐ Document what works and what doesn't

Let's explore how to build your first automation using these patterns...

## BUILDING YOUR FIRST AUTOMATION

The journey to automation begins with a single workflow. Rather than trying to automate everything at once, successful content creators start with one specific process that will save them significant time and energy.

### Choosing Your Starting Point

The best first automation solves a clear, specific problem in your content workflow. Look for tasks that are:

- Repetitive and predictable
- Currently taking significant time
- Following consistent steps
- Not requiring complex creative decisions

For example, a book publisher might notice they spend hours formatting manuscripts and creating marketing descriptions. A digital asset creator might be manually resizing designs for different marketplaces. A blogger might be copying posts from their writing tool to WordPress, then manually adding images and tags.

The ideal starting point has clear triggers and desired outcomes. When you save a final draft (trigger), you want it formatted and posted as a draft in WordPress (outcome). When you complete a design (trigger), you want it resized and listed on multiple marketplaces (outcome). These clear cause-and-effect relationships make perfect automation candidates.

Avoid starting with tasks that require nuanced creative decisions or complex human judgment. For instance, don't try to automate your entire content creation process first. Instead, automate the parts that happen after content creation - the formatting, the distribution, the tracking.

Think about your current workflow. Where do you find yourself saying "I always have to..." or "Every time I finish a piece, I need to..."? These phrases often point to perfect automation opportunities.

**Setting Up Your Tools**

Before diving into workflow creation, let's set up your automation toolkit properly. While there are many automation tools available, we'll start with Zapier - it's user-friendly, reliable, and perfect for your first automations.

Start by creating a free Zapier account. While paid plans offer more features, the free tier lets you build your first automations and learn the basics. As you visit Zapier's site, you'll notice they offer templates - bookmark these for later, but we'll start from scratch to understand the process fully.

Next, connect the core services you'll use in your automation. For a basic content publishing workflow, this typically means:

- Your content creation tool (Google Docs, Notion, etc.)
- Your publishing platform (WordPress, Medium, etc.)
- Any middleware tools (image handling, formatting tools)

Take time to verify each connection. Zapier will guide you through authenticating each service, and it's crucial to ensure these connections are solid before building your workflow. Think of these connections as the foundation of your automation house - they need to be sturdy.

A common mistake is rushing this setup phase. Resist the urge to start building workflows immediately. Instead, familiarize yourself with each tool's triggers and actions. What can each service watch for? What actions can it take? Understanding these capabilities will help you design better automations.

**Creating Your First Workflow**

Let's build a simple but powerful automation that takes your content from creation to publication-ready. We'll use the Trigger-Action-Result pattern you learned earlier, keeping things focused and reliable.

Your automation journey begins with selecting a trigger - the event that starts your workflow. In Zapier's interface, click "Create Zap" and you'll see a vast library of possible triggers. For content systems, the most useful triggers are typically new files or documents. You might watch for new files in a Google Drive folder, new tagged documents in Notion, or completed drafts in Google Docs.

For your first automation, we recommend starting with Google Drive as your trigger. It's reliable, well-documented, and Zapier's own tutorials (found at zapier.com/learn) provide excellent step-by-step guidance for setting this up.

Next comes your action - what happens when that trigger fires. While Zapier can handle complex sequences, start with a single, clear transformation. A classic example is moving content from Google Docs to WordPress. This specific automation is covered in detail in Zapier's "From Google Docs to WordPress" guide in their help center.

Before building any automation, spend 30 minutes exploring Zapier's learning resources:

- Start with their "Getting Started with Zapier" course
- Watch their workflow tutorials on YouTube
- Join their active Facebook community for tips
- Bookmark their help center articles for your chosen tools

When testing your first workflow, follow these essential steps:

1. Send a test document through the system
2. Check that formatting transfers correctly
3. Verify that images and links survive the journey
4. Confirm the draft appears as expected in WordPress

Remember: your first automation doesn't need to be perfect. Even a basic workflow that moves content and preserves formatting can save you 15-20 minutes per piece. That's valuable time you can spend creating more content or planning your next automation enhancement.

**Testing and Troubleshooting**

The difference between a reliable content system and a constant headache often comes down to how well you test and troubleshoot your automations. Let's build these skills systematically.

Before sending real content through your automation, create a testing protocol. Start with a test document that includes everything your content typically contains: headings, images, links, formatting, and any special characters. Zapier's testing feature lets you run your automation with this document without actually publishing anything - take advantage of this safe environment.

When testing, watch for these common issues:

1. Formatting inconsistencies (especially with headers and lists)
2. Image transfer problems
3. Broken or malformed links
4. Special character encoding issues
5. Metadata loss (like titles or categories)

Zapier provides detailed logging for each step of your automation. Learn to read these logs - they're your best friend when troubleshooting. In your Zapier dashboard, click on any recent automation run to see exactly what happened at each step. This helps pinpoint where things might be going wrong.

For ongoing reliability, set up a few simple safeguards. Create a dedicated test folder for your trigger and enable Zapier's error notifications. Keep a small test document ready for quick checks, and maintain a log of any issues you encounter and their solutions. This documentation will prove invaluable as your system grows.

When something does go wrong (and it will), don't panic. Most issues are predictable and solvable. Authentication problems can usually be fixed by reconnecting your services. Format mismatches might require adjusting your content template. Trigger timing issues often come down to folder permissions, and data mapping errors typically need a quick review of your field connections.

The Zapier community forums are invaluable for troubleshooting. Before spending hours solving a problem, search there - chances are someone else has encountered and solved it already.

**Growing Your First Automation**

Once your basic automation is running smoothly, you're ready to enhance it thoughtfully. The key is adding capability in small, testable increments rather than making sweeping changes.

Start by identifying one small enhancement that would make your workflow more valuable. For example, if you're moving content from Google Docs to WordPress, you might want to automatically generate featured images using AI. Before diving in, spend time in Zapier's "Connecting AI Tools" guide (found in their help center) to understand the best practices for integrating AI services.

A natural next step is adding quality checks to your workflow. Zapier can integrate with tools like Grammarly's API or custom AI endpoints for content verification. While setting up these integrations requires some technical knowledge, Zapier's "Working with APIs" course provides an excellent foundation for understanding these more advanced connections.

As your automation grows more sophisticated, you'll want to learn about Zapier's Paths feature, which lets your workflow make decisions based on content characteristics. For instance, your system could route different types of content through different formatting processes. The "Advanced Zaps" section of Zapier's learning portal covers this functionality in detail.

Consider adding these enhancements gradually:

1. Basic metadata handling (titles, categories, tags)
2. Image processing and optimization
3. Quality check integrations
4. Conditional formatting paths
5. Analytics tracking

Remember that each addition should be thoroughly tested before moving to the next. Keep your test document updated to include examples of everything your enhanced automation needs to handle. When you're ready to learn more advanced techniques, Zapier's monthly webinars offer deep dives into specific automation scenarios.

The goal isn't to build the most complex automation possible - it's to create a reliable system that saves you time and maintains quality. Let your actual needs drive the growth of your automation, and always keep documentation of your enhancements for future reference.

### ACTION ITEMS

- ☐ Pick your simplest repetitive task
- ☐ Map the exact steps involved
- ☐ Choose appropriate tools
- ☐ Build a basic automation
- ☐ Test with sample content
- ☐ Monitor and adjust as needed
- ☐ Document the entire process

## REAL SYSTEM EXAMPLES

Let's explore three real-world content systems and see how they use automation to operate efficiently. Each demonstrates different automation patterns while maintaining quality and scalability.

## Automated Book Publishing System

Every morning at 10am, Make triggers GPT-4 to generate three fresh book concepts based on your chosen genre and style preferences, sending them to your phone via Telegram for quick approval. This system shines with non-fiction - think how-to guides, educational content, and topic-specific handbooks. While it can assist with fiction (generating ideas and outlines), narrative work still needs significant human creativity.

From there, the automation loop begins. For each chapter, the system:

1. Generates a detailed chapter outline
2. Creates an initial draft using GPT-4 or Claude
3. Runs it through multiple AI iterations for improvement
4. Saves each version in Google Docs
5. Moves to the next chapter when you approve

The system maintains momentum by sending you daily progress updates and only requesting input at key decision points. When all chapters are complete, it initiates a comprehensive quality control sequence:

- AI-powered consistency check across chapters
- ProWritingAid for grammar and style
- Genre-specific checks (like romance beat analysis or mystery plot verification)
- Character voice consistency validation
- Pacing analysis

Meanwhile, DALL-E or Midjourney generates cover options based on successful books in your genre, and GPT-4 crafts multiple versions of book descriptions and marketing copy. The system stores everything in an organized project folder, with each element (manuscript, covers, descriptions) in its own subfolder.

When you're ready for review, you can interact with the manuscript through a simple interface that lets you query the AI about specific plot points, character arcs, or potential improvements.

After approval, Make triggers the formatting sequence. For this crucial step, you have several options. You can:

- Use Calibre's command-line tools to automatically convert your manuscript to multiple formats (EPUB, MOBI, PDF)
- Set up a Google Docs template that's pre-formatted for KDP's requirements
- Use specialized tools like Vellum (if you're on Mac) or Atticus that can automate formatting
- Consider Draft2Digital's conversion tools which can handle multiple publishing platforms

The system then automatically:

- Generates both ebook and print-ready PDF versions
- Creates preview files for different platforms
- Prepares the complete KDP publishing package
- Sets up your publishing metadata across platforms

Choose the formatting approach that fits your workflow - the key is making it repeatable and reliable. Some authors prefer the control of a well-designed template, while others opt for full automation through tools like Calibre.

**Automated Digital Asset Factory**

Picture a design system that never sleeps. Every night at midnight, Make scans your "Template Ideas" Notion database, where you've been collecting inspiration and market research. The system uses GPT-4 to analyze trending design needs and DALL-E to generate initial concept sketches, presenting you with three promising directions each morning via Slack.

Once you approve a direction, the automation chain begins. First, AI generates the base template design in Figma, then your custom style guide automatically applies to ensure brand consistency. The system then creates variations across multiple dimensions: color schemes ranging from brand colors to seasonal palettes, sizes for every platform from social media to print, and style variations from minimal to playful.

Quality control flows naturally through several layers. AI checks fundamental design principles like contrast and spacing, while automated tools verify accessibility standards and brand guideline compliance. Every asset undergoes resolution and format validation before moving forward.

The distribution system then takes the reins, creating preview images for each marketplace while GPT-4 generates compelling product descriptions. The system intelligently tags assets based on their design elements and potential uses, then lists them across Creative Market, Etsy, and Gumroad, with pricing automatically adjusted based on marketplace analytics.

Beyond publication, the system continues its work. It monitors sales and engagement metrics, suggesting new variations based on popular items. It automatically generates social media content to showcase your designs and even creates targeted ads using your highest-performing assets.

**Automated YouTube Facts Channel**

Picture a simple but effective system that runs a facts-based YouTube channel while you sleep. Every morning at 8am, Make checks your "Video Topics" Airtable base, where you store interesting fact collections you've researched. For today's scheduled video - let's say "10 Fascinating Space Facts" - the automation begins its work.

First, the content pipeline kicks in. Using your pre-written prompt templates, GPT-4:

- Structures the facts into a clear script
- Adds engaging transitions between facts
- Generates video descriptions and tags
- Creates timestamps for each fact

The video creation process then starts automatically. This is where you'll need to do some research - the automated video creation space is evolving rapidly, with new tools launching frequently. Search

Zapier's integrations directory for "video creation" and compare the latest options. Look for tools that can:

- Convert scripts to voiceover using AI narration
- Handle stock footage integration
- Support captions and overlays
- Offer template systems
- Integrate well with automation platforms

While the video processes, the upload automation handles YouTube prep:

- Bannerbear automatically generates thumbnail variations using:

    - Your preset YouTube thumbnail template
    - The video title as dynamic text
    - Your brand colors and fonts
    - Different layouts you've pre-configured

- Using YouTube's API (through Zapier or Make), the system:

    - Uploads the video as unlisted
    - Sets descriptions and tags
    - Assigns playlists
    - Configures end screens
    - Schedules publication time

Once uploaded, Make sends you a quick Slack notification to review it. After your approval (just a single click), the automation changes the video's visibility to public and schedules it for your next posting slot.

The system then monitors basic metrics:

- View count in first 24 hours
- Audience retention drops
- Comment notifications
- Basic analytics alerts

This system isn't complex, but it works - taking what could be a 4-hour video production process down to about 30 minutes of oversight. Most importantly, you can build this entire workflow using tools available today, even as specific tools evolve and improve.

## SCALING AND MAINTENANCE

As your content system grows more sophisticated, maintaining its reliability becomes crucial. Start by establishing good monitoring habits. Set up notification systems that alert you to both successes and failures - a quick Slack message when content publishes successfully, and immediate alerts if something goes wrong. Tools like Make and Zapier provide detailed logs of each automation run, helping you spot patterns and potential issues before they become problems.

When failures occur (and they will), having a graceful handling system makes all the difference. Build pause points into your automation where content can safely wait if a downstream system fails. For example, if your video rendering service is temporarily down, your script generation can complete and wait in a holding folder. Set up retry logic for transient failures, and ensure your system maintains a clear record of where each piece of content is in the pipeline.

Resist the urge to add complexity until it's truly needed. Each new feature or condition in your automation creates another potential point of failure. Instead of building elaborate error handling up front, start with simple, reliable workflows and add sophistication only when you encounter actual problems. Let real usage patterns guide your system's evolution.

Documentation becomes your best friend as your system grows. Create a simple operations manual that outlines:

- How each automation works
- Where to find logs and monitoring tools
- Common failure points and their solutions
- Regular maintenance tasks and schedules

Most importantly, document your system's dependencies. When a service updates its API or changes its features, you'll want to quickly identify which parts of your automation might be affected. Keep a running log of any adjustments you make - this history often reveals patterns that help with future improvements.

Remember: a reliable, simple system is far more valuable than a complex one that requires constant attention. Focus on building stable foundations that can grow with your needs.

> **ACTION ITEMS**
>
> ☐ Create your system documentation
> ☐ Set up basic monitoring alerts
> ☐ Document all system dependencies
> ☐ Create a backup procedure
> ☐ Test failure recovery process
> ☐ Schedule regular maintenance checks

## LEARNING PATH AND RESOURCES

Your automation journey doesn't end with building your first system. The field evolves rapidly, and staying current helps you build better, more reliable content systems. Start by mastering the fundamentals through Zapier's free courses and Make's getting started guides. Both platforms offer excellent tutorials that teach automation thinking alongside practical skills.

Communities are invaluable for learning and troubleshooting. Join the Zapier Community forum and Make's official community - both are filled with creators sharing workflows and solving common problems. Reddit's r/automation and r/zapier subreddits offer additional perspectives and real-world examples. When you encounter issues, search these communities first - chances are someone else has already solved your problem.

As you learn, watch out for common pitfalls. Don't try to automate everything at once - start with simple, reliable workflows and expand gradually. Avoid building overly complex systems just because you can; sometimes a simple two-step automation is more valuable than an elaborate multi-path workflow. Always maintain manual backup procedures for critical processes, and test new automations thoroughly before relying on them.

For hands-on learning, start with these practical exercises:

1. Build a simple content distribution workflow
2. Create a basic monitoring system
3. Set up error notifications
4. Practice recovering from common failures

When you're ready to advance, explore API documentation for your key services. Understanding APIs opens up powerful customization options. Consider learning basic scripting - even simple JavaScript or Python knowledge can dramatically expand what your automations can do.

Remember that automation is a journey, not a destination. Your systems will evolve as tools improve and your needs change. Stay curious, keep learning, and most importantly - keep building. The best way to learn is by creating real systems that solve real problems.

## Distribution & Monetization

Building a content system is one thing - making it profitable is another. The key to successful monetization lies in smart distribution across multiple platforms, each configured to generate revenue in different ways. Start with platforms that align with your content type: marketplaces like Gumroad or Etsy for digital products, Medium's Partner Program for articles, or YouTube's Partner Program for videos.

Your automation can handle much of the distribution work. Set up your system to automatically format content for each platform's requirements. A single piece of content might flow through Make to become a blog post on your website, a condensed version for

Medium, key points for Twitter threads, and a newsletter version for Substack.

Payment processing should be as hands-off as possible. Tools like Stripe and PayPal offer robust APIs that integrate well with automation platforms. Your system can automatically generate and send invoices, process recurring subscriptions, handle refund requests, update customer access permissions, and send payment confirmation emails without your intervention.

Multiple revenue streams provide stability. Beyond direct sales, consider affiliate links that your content system can automatically insert, sponsored content opportunities tracked through your CRM, premium memberships managed through automated access systems, and digital product upsells suggested based on purchase history.

Analytics become crucial as you scale. Configure your automation to track revenue per platform, content performance metrics, customer acquisition costs, conversion rates, and engagement patterns. Let your system generate weekly summaries highlighting top-performing content, revenue trends, platform-specific metrics, and customer feedback patterns.

Most importantly, use these insights to refine your system. When certain content types consistently perform better, adjust your automation to produce more of what works. When specific platforms show higher returns, prioritize distribution to those channels. Remember: monetization should feel natural to your audience. Focus on providing value first, and let your automation handle the mechanics of turning that value into revenue.

> **ACTION ITEMS**
>
> ☐ Choose your primary distribution platforms
> ☐ Set up payment processing automation
> ☐ Configure analytics tracking
> ☐ Create revenue reporting system
> ☐ Plan content adaptation workflows
> ☐ Test payment processing security

**Growth & Optimization**

Once your content system is running smoothly, growth becomes an exercise in careful expansion rather than radical change. Start by exploring new content verticals that complement your existing work. If your system successfully produces how-to guides, it might naturally expand into video tutorials or downloadable worksheets. Let your audience's needs guide these expansions, not just the technical possibilities.

A/B testing becomes your compass for optimization. Set up your system to automatically test different approaches: varying content lengths, testing different posting times, or experimenting with format styles. The key is testing one element at a time and letting data drive your decisions. Your automation can track these experiments and alert you when significant patterns emerge.

Performance analytics should inform every growth decision. Configure your system to monitor not just basic metrics like views and sales, but deeper patterns like content topic performance, platform-specific engagement rates, and revenue per content type. Look for unexpected successes – sometimes your most profitable opportunities come from surprising directions.

When expanding to new platforms, resist the urge to rush in. Start by having your system cross-post existing content in platform-appropriate formats. Monitor the response, engage with the audience, and only then consider creating platform-specific content. Remember that each new platform adds complexity to your system – make sure the potential return justifies the effort.

Perhaps most importantly, know when to add human oversight. While automation can handle tremendous scale, certain growth points benefit from human judgment. Creative decisions, strategic shifts, and community management often need a personal touch. Design your system to flag situations where human insight adds real value, rather than requiring oversight of every process.

The most successful content systems grow organically, driven by audience response and clear metrics rather than just technical capabilities. Let your system's data guide your expansion while maintaining the quality and reliability that made it successful in the first place.

---

**ACTION ITEMS**

- ☐ Set up A/B testing framework
- ☐ Create performance tracking metrics
- ☐ Plan expansion roadmap
- ☐ Document optimization process
- ☐ Configure growth analytics
- ☐ Establish review checkpoints

---

## Chapter Summary

You've just learned how to build automated content systems that can work while you sleep. The key takeaway? Start simple but think big. Begin with a basic automation - perhaps that YouTube facts channel or social media template system we explored - and grow it thoughtfully. Remember that the goal isn't to remove humans from the creative process, but to automate the repetitive tasks that drain your creative energy.

Your next steps are straightforward:

1. Choose one content type to automate (video, templates, articles)
2. Set up a basic Zapier or Make account
3. Build a simple two-step automation
4. Test thoroughly before scaling
5. Add capabilities gradually as you learn

In the next chapter, we'll explore how to use AI for content research and idea generation. You'll learn how to build systems that not only create content but discover opportunities and trends automatically. Your content factory is about to get a lot smarter.

For now, focus on getting that first automation running. Keep it simple, make it reliable, and watch how it transforms your content creation process. The most powerful content systems all started with a single automated step.

### KEY TAKEAWAYS

- Start with one simple, reliable automation rather than trying to build complex systems immediately
- Focus on automating repetitive tasks while keeping human oversight for creative decisions
- Build content systems around three core elements: content generation, distribution, and monetization
- Choose automation patterns (Trigger-Action-Result, Monitor-Alert-Respond, Create-Transform-Distribute) based on specific workflow needs
- Test thoroughly before scaling - every automation should be reliable before adding complexity
- Document your systems, including dependencies, common issues, and maintenance procedures
- Use integration platforms like Zapier or Make as the foundation for connecting different tools and services
- Implement quality control checkpoints throughout your automated workflows
- Monitor system performance through clear metrics and analytics
- Build feedback loops that help your system improve over time
- Create multiple revenue streams across different platforms for stability
- Start with platforms that align naturally with your content type
- Let audience response and data guide system expansion rather than technical possibilities
- Maintain manual backup procedures for critical processes
- Keep learning and staying current with automation tools and possibilities

CHAPTER 8

# Prompt Engineering Services

Imagine having a client pay you $500 for a single prompt. Not because it's long or complex, but because it saves their team 20 hours every week. This isn't fiction - it's the reality of professional prompt engineering services.

Welcome to one of the most overlooked opportunities in the AI landscape. While everyone else is sharing basic prompts in Twitter threads, you're about to learn how to build systematic, tested prompt engineering services that solve real business problems.

The opportunity is unique: Companies are investing heavily in AI tools but struggling to get consistent results. Their teams waste hours with trial-and-error prompting. Every prompt that doesn't work perfectly costs them time and money. This is where you come in - not with random prompts, but with engineered solutions that actually work.

In this chapter, you'll learn how to build prompt engineering services that companies genuinely need. We'll explore everything from developing testing frameworks to packaging your services. Most importantly, you'll see how to turn prompt engineering from a skill into a systematic business.

Let's start by understanding what makes prompt engineering valuable...

## Understanding the Market

The prompt engineering services market is still young but growing rapidly. While casual users share basic prompts online, businesses need something more reliable: systematically designed prompts that consistently deliver results.

The market naturally divides into four main service types. Prompt optimization focuses on improving existing prompts - making them more efficient, reliable, and consistent. Custom prompt development involves building new systems from scratch, often creating chains of prompts that work together for complex workflows. Training and documentation helps teams understand and implement prompt engineering effectively, while ongoing support ensures prompts keep performing as AI models and business needs evolve.

The demand comes from diverse but specific business needs. Marketing agencies need prompts that maintain consistent brand voice across massive content operations. E-commerce companies want to automate product descriptions while maintaining quality. Enterprise teams seek to streamline their documentation and training materials. Software companies need help automating everything from API documentation to support responses.

The most profitable opportunities aren't in selling individual prompts - they're in solving business problems systematically. Companies are looking for efficiency systems that reduce manual work, consistency solutions that maintain quality at scale, and frameworks that enable entire teams to use AI effectively.

This value-driven market supports several pricing models. Project-based fees range from $500 to $2000 for custom prompt systems, based on complexity and business value. Monthly retainers of $1000-5000 provide ongoing optimization and support. Individual prompt optimization might cost $100-500, with higher rates for complex workflows. Training and consultation typically runs $200-500 per hour.

The key to pricing is focusing on business value rather than time spent. A single well-engineered prompt that saves a team 10 hours per week is worth thousands to the right client. Package and price your services based on the problems you solve, not the time you spend solving them.

> **ACTION ITEMS**
>
> - ☐ Research local businesses using AI tools
> - ☐ Identify 3 common prompt-related pain points
> - ☐ List potential target industries
> - ☐ Research current market rates
> - ☐ Define your initial service offerings
> - ☐ Create a competitive analysis
> - ☐ Document unique value proposition

## Building Your Service Foundation

Professional prompt engineering isn't about writing clever prompts - it's about building reliable systems that consistently deliver results. Your foundation needs to be methodical, tested, and documented. This is what separates professional services from casual prompt sharing.

Start by mastering core prompt engineering principles. Learn how different AI models respond to various prompt structures. Understand the impact of context, the importance of clear constraints, and how to handle edge cases. Most importantly, develop a systematic approach to prompt development that you can replicate across projects.

Testing is where professional prompt engineering truly shines. Develop a rigorous testing methodology that validates prompts across different scenarios. Your testing should verify not just that prompts work, but that they work consistently and handle unexpected inputs gracefully. Create test cases that mirror real-world usage, and document both successes and failures.

Documentation becomes your competitive advantage. Every prompt should have clear documentation explaining its purpose, requirements, and limitations. Build templates that capture not just the prompt itself, but its context, testing history, and known issues.

This documentation becomes invaluable as you scale your services and work with larger clients.

Quality assurance ties everything together. Develop frameworks for measuring prompt performance against specific metrics. Track token usage, response consistency, and error rates. Build systems for monitoring prompt performance over time, especially as AI models update and business needs evolve.

The goal isn't perfection - it's reliability and repeatability. Your clients aren't buying prompts; they're buying confidence that their AI interactions will work consistently. Build your foundation with this in mind, creating systems and processes that you can trust and scale.

### ACTION ITEMS

- ☐ Create your prompt testing framework
- ☐ Set up documentation templates
- ☐ Build a prompt version control system
- ☐ Establish quality metrics
- ☐ Create client reporting templates
- ☐ Set up performance tracking tools
- ☐ Document your development process

### Service Packages

Success in prompt engineering services comes from packaging your expertise in ways that solve real business problems. Rather than offering generic prompt writing, create focused service packages that deliver specific, measurable value.

Start with prompt optimization - the perfect entry point for many clients. Companies often come to you with existing prompts that almost work but need refinement. You'll analyze their current prompts, identify inefficiencies, and rebuild them for better performance. This might mean reducing token usage, improving consistency, or adding error handling. It's a concrete service with clear before-and-after results.

Custom prompt development takes things further. Here, you're building complete prompt systems from scratch. A client might need a workflow for generating product descriptions, analyzing customer feedback, or automating support responses. You'll develop not just individual prompts, but entire chains of prompts working together. This includes testing frameworks, documentation, and implementation guides.

Training and consultation help clients build internal capabilities. Some companies want to develop their own prompt engineering expertise. You'll create custom workshops, develop best practices guides, and help teams understand prompt engineering principles. This isn't just teaching - it's helping clients build their own systematic approaches to AI implementation.

Ongoing support ensures long-term success. AI models update, business needs evolve, and prompts need maintenance. Monthly retainers cover prompt optimization, performance monitoring, and regular updates. You become a trusted advisor, helping clients adapt and improve their prompt systems over time.

Package these services based on client needs and goals. Some clients need quick optimization, others want complete systems, and many benefit from combining services. The key is presenting clear solutions to specific problems, priced according to the value they deliver.

> **ACTION ITEMS**
> 
> ☐ Define your core service packages
> ☐ Set package pricing tiers
> ☐ Create service deliverables list
> ☐ Write package descriptions
> ☐ Define scope for each service
> ☐ Create sample timelines
> ☐ List package limitations

## Implementation Examples

Let's explore how prompt engineering services work in the real world, starting with a marketing agency case. Imagine an agency struggling with consistent brand voice across dozens of weekly blog posts. You develop a systematic prompt chain that first analyzes their best-performing content, then creates a brand voice framework, and finally generates content that maintains that voice. The result? Content creation time cut in half while maintaining consistent quality.

E-commerce product descriptions showcase another powerful application. A client selling thousands of products needs unique, SEO-friendly descriptions at scale. Your prompt system doesn't just generate descriptions - it analyzes top-performing listings, incorporates category-specific keywords, and maintains brand tone. More importantly, it includes quality checks that flag potential issues for review. What once took weeks now happens overnight.

Customer service automation demonstrates the value of sophisticated prompt engineering. Rather than simple response templates, you build an intelligent system that analyzes customer inquiries, categorizes issues, and generates appropriate responses. The system knows when to provide direct answers, when to escalate to human agents, and how to maintain a consistent support voice.

Support teams see their response times drop while satisfaction scores rise.

Content generation systems show how different prompt types work together. For a client needing regular social media content, you create a system that generates ideas, writes posts, suggests hashtags, and even predicts optimal posting times. The prompts work in sequence, each building on the previous output while maintaining brand guidelines and engagement goals.

These aren't theoretical examples - they're based on real business needs and deliver measurable results. The key isn't just writing prompts; it's building systems that solve specific business problems reliably and at scale.

## Delivery Systems

Delivering prompt engineering services professionally requires more than just writing good prompts. You need systematic approaches that ensure consistent quality and clear communication with clients. Think of your delivery system as a well-oiled machine that turns client needs into tested, documented solutions.

Client onboarding sets the tone for everything that follows. Create a streamlined process that captures essential information about your client's needs, current challenges, and success metrics. Use questionnaires that guide clients through describing their use cases, sharing existing prompts, and defining what success looks like. This initial clarity prevents misunderstandings and ensures you're solving the right problems.

Your testing workflow becomes your quality guarantee. Each prompt goes through rigorous testing that simulates real-world usage. Test with different inputs, edge cases, and potential failure points. Document everything - not just what works, but what doesn't. This testing history becomes invaluable when explaining your development process to clients and handling future optimizations.

Results documentation proves your value. Create clear before-and-after comparisons showing improvements in efficiency, consistency, or quality. Build dashboards that track key metrics like time saved, error rates reduced, or output quality improved. Make complex improvements tangible and understandable to non-technical stakeholders.

The iteration process keeps solutions improving over time. Schedule regular check-ins to gather feedback, analyze performance, and make adjustments. Build systems for tracking prompt performance in production and flagging areas for improvement. Your delivery system should make ongoing optimization feel natural and valuable to clients.

> **ACTION ITEMS**
>
> ☐ Create client onboarding questionnaire
> ☐ Set up project management system
> ☐ Build testing documentation templates
> ☐ Create progress reporting system
> ☐ Establish communication protocols
> ☐ Define revision processes
> ☐ Create delivery templates

### Growth & Scaling

Growing a prompt engineering service isn't about working more hours - it's about leveraging your expertise and results systematically. Each successful project becomes a foundation for attracting better clients and delivering more valuable services.

Your portfolio tells your success story. Document every significant improvement you achieve for clients. That marketing agency whose content creation time dropped by 50%? That's not just a project - it's proof of your expertise. Build detailed case studies that show both your technical skills and business impact. Focus on metrics that matter: time saved, quality improved, costs reduced.

Case studies become your most powerful sales tool. Don't just list what you did - tell the story of the problem, your solution, and the results. Show how you approached the challenge, what systems you built, and how you measured success. These stories resonate with potential clients facing similar challenges. They see not just what you can do, but how you think and solve problems.

Referral systems multiply your growth naturally. Happy clients become your best advocates, but only if you make it easy for them. Create simple ways for clients to share their success stories. Build partnerships with complementary service providers - AI consultants, marketing agencies, or business efficiency experts who can recommend your services to their clients.

Service expansion follows natural paths. As you work with clients, you'll spot patterns in their needs. Maybe your product description clients need help with customer service prompts. Perhaps your marketing clients need training for their teams. Let your expansion be guided by real demand, building new service offerings that complement your existing expertise.

### ACTION ITEMS

- ☐ Create portfolio documentation system
- ☐ Set up case study template
- ☐ Build referral tracking system
- ☐ Create partnership outreach plan
- ☐ Define growth metrics
- ☐ Plan service expansion roadmap
- ☐ Create scaling procedures

## Chapter Summary

You've just learned how to build a professional prompt engineering service that delivers real value to businesses. The key isn't just writing better prompts - it's building systematic approaches to solving business problems through prompt engineering. Your expertise becomes valuable when it's packaged into reliable, repeatable systems that deliver measurable results.

Start small but think systematically. Begin with prompt optimization services for a single client, documenting your process and results carefully. Build your testing frameworks and quality assurance systems as you go. Each project teaches you something new about what businesses need and how to deliver it effectively.

Your next steps are straightforward: identify a specific type of client you want to serve, develop your systematic approach to solving their problems, and create your first service package. Focus on delivering measurable value and documenting your results. Remember, you're not selling prompts - you're selling solutions to business problems.

In the next chapter, we'll explore AI Business Consultation, where you'll learn how to help companies implement AI strategically across their operations. The prompt engineering expertise you've developed here will become a valuable part of your broader AI consulting toolkit.

For now, focus on building your first prompt engineering service package. The businesses struggling with AI implementation need your systematic approach more than they realize.

## KEY TAKEAWAYS

- Focus on solving specific business problems rather than selling individual prompts
- Price based on business value delivered (time/money saved) rather than time spent
- Build systematic testing frameworks to ensure prompt reliability and consistency
- Create comprehensive documentation for all prompts, including context and limitations
- Package services strategically: optimization, custom development, training, and ongoing support
- Develop rigorous quality assurance processes to maintain consistent results
- Start with prompt optimization services as an entry point with clear before/after results
- Create detailed case studies showing concrete business impact and metrics
- Build referral systems and partnerships to grow sustainably
- Document everything - process, testing, results, and improvements
- Implement thorough client onboarding to understand needs and define success metrics
- Monitor prompt performance over time, especially as AI models update
- Focus on serving specific client types rather than trying to help everyone
- Build repeatable systems that can scale with your business
- Maintain ongoing relationships through retainers and support services

CHAPTER 9

# AI Business Consultation

Every day, businesses are told they need to implement AI or risk falling behind. But for most companies, especially small and medium-sized businesses, the path forward isn't clear. They don't need high-level AI strategy or complex technical implementations - they need practical guidance on how to use AI effectively in their specific business context.

This creates a unique opportunity for side hustlers with AI experience. You don't need to be a technical expert or have an AI degree. What businesses really need is someone who understands both AI's practical capabilities and real-world business operations. They need a guide who can help them navigate the AI landscape and implement solutions that actually work.

Think about it: You've learned how to use AI tools effectively. You understand prompt engineering, automation possibilities, and how to build reliable systems. More importantly, you know how to apply these capabilities to solve real business problems. This knowledge, combined with your business experience, is exactly what companies are looking for.

The timing is perfect for starting an AI consultation side hustle. Companies are past the initial AI hype and looking for practical implementation help. They don't want theoretical discussions about AI potential - they want someone who can show them how to use AI tools to save time, reduce costs, and improve operations today.

In this chapter, you'll learn how to package your AI knowledge into valuable consultation services. We'll explore how to assess business needs, develop practical solutions, and deliver real value to clients. Most importantly, you'll see how to build this as a side hustle that works alongside your existing career.

## Understanding the Market

The market for AI consultation isn't about Fortune 500 companies with massive AI budgets. It's about the millions of small and medium-sized businesses trying to figure out how AI fits into their operations. These companies don't need enterprise AI strategies - they need practical help implementing tools that can make a difference today.

Most businesses approach AI implementation backwards. They start by asking what AI can do, rather than identifying specific business problems AI could solve. This leads to unfocused efforts, wasted resources, and disappointment with results. Your role is to help them flip this approach: start with their business challenges, then identify where AI can make a meaningful difference.

The most common challenges businesses face aren't technical - they're practical. How to reduce repetitive tasks without sacrificing quality. How to maintain consistent customer service while scaling operations. How to create content efficiently while maintaining brand voice. These are the problems keeping business owners up at night, and they're exactly the kinds of challenges that well-implemented AI can help solve.

What clients really want isn't AI expertise - it's business results. They want someone who can:

- Show them specific ways AI can improve their operations
- Help them choose the right tools for their needs
- Guide them through implementation without disrupting their business
- Ensure their team actually uses the new tools effectively
- Demonstrate clear return on their AI investment

This creates a perfect opportunity for positioning your services. Rather than competing with technical AI consultants or enterprise strategy firms, position yourself as the practical implementation guide. You're not selling AI - you're selling business improvement through targeted AI implementation.

Your market sweet spot is businesses that:

- Are large enough to invest in improvement but not large enough for full-time AI staff
- Have clear operational challenges that AI could help solve
- Want practical results rather than cutting-edge technology
- Need guidance but not complete outsourcing

This positioning lets you focus on what you do best: helping businesses implement AI tools effectively to solve real problems. You're not promising AI transformation - you're delivering practical improvements that make a measurable difference to their bottom line.

### ACTION ITEMS

- ☐ Define your target business size/type
- ☐ List 5 common business problems you can solve
- ☐ Research local businesses in your target market
- ☐ Document your unique value proposition
- ☐ Identify your competitive advantages
- ☐ Set initial consultation rates
- ☐ Create your service boundaries

### Your Consultation Foundation

Success as an AI consultant isn't about knowing every AI tool and technique - it's about building systematic approaches to solving business problems. Your foundation needs to be practical, repeatable, and focused on delivering real value to clients.

Start by organizing your knowledge base around business problems rather than AI capabilities. Understand how AI can improve customer service, streamline content creation, automate repetitive tasks, or enhance decision-making. Build a library of case studies and examples showing how different tools solve specific challenges. This problem-first approach helps you match solutions to client needs effectively.

Your assessment framework becomes your secret weapon. Develop a systematic way to evaluate a business's current operations, identify AI opportunities, and prioritize implementations. This isn't about complex technical assessments - it's about understanding workflow bottlenecks, time-consuming tasks, and areas where consistency or scale are challenging. Your framework should help clients see exactly where AI can make the biggest impact.

Solution blueprints save you from reinventing the wheel with each client. Create templates for common implementations: customer service automation, content workflows, data analysis systems, or document processing. Each blueprint should include tool recommendations, implementation steps, and expected outcomes. These aren't rigid plans - they're starting points you can customize for each client's specific needs.

Documentation becomes your competitive advantage. Build clear, practical guides for everything from tool setup to team training. Focus on making complex concepts understandable and actionable. Your documentation should help clients maintain and optimize their AI implementations long after your initial work is done.

The goal isn't to become an AI expert in every domain - it's to build reliable systems for helping businesses implement AI effectively. Your foundation should make it easy to assess needs, recommend solutions, and guide implementation consistently. This systematic approach lets you deliver value efficiently while building a sustainable consulting practice.

## ACTION ITEMS

- ☐ Create your business assessment template
- ☐ Build solution blueprint library
- ☐ Develop implementation guides
- ☐ Set up document templates
- ☐ Create client questionnaires
- ☐ Build tool recommendation list
- ☐ Document your methodology

### Service Packages

Success in AI consultation comes from packaging your expertise in ways that solve specific business problems. Rather than offering generic AI consulting, create focused services that deliver clear, measurable value. Your service packages should guide clients from understanding AI opportunities to implementing solutions that actually work.

Start with AI Readiness Assessment - it's the perfect entry point for most clients. This initial service examines their current operations, identifies AI opportunities, and provides clear recommendations. You're not just listing where AI could help; you're showing them exactly where to start for the biggest impact. This assessment often leads naturally to deeper engagements as clients see the specific value you can deliver.

Implementation Planning takes things further. Once clients understand their opportunities, they need a clear path forward. Your implementation plans outline specific tools, steps, and timelines. Include cost estimates, resource requirements, and expected outcomes. This isn't just a technical plan - it's a business roadmap that shows exactly how AI will improve their operations.

Tool Selection and Setup becomes a natural next step. Many clients get overwhelmed by the array of AI tools available. Your service helps them choose the right tools for their needs, then ensures these tools are set up correctly. This includes creating proper workflows, establishing quality control measures, and integrating with existing systems.

Team Training ensures AI implementations actually get used. Develop training programs that focus on practical application rather than technical details. Show teams how AI tools make their jobs easier, not more complicated. Include real examples from their work, clear documentation, and ongoing support resources.

Ongoing Advisory services provide continued value as clients grow with AI. Monthly retainers might include regular check-ins, optimization reviews, and guidance on new opportunities. You become a trusted advisor helping them stay current with AI developments and maintain effective implementations.

Package these services based on client needs and goals. Some clients need comprehensive support from assessment through implementation. Others might want focused help with specific aspects. Price your packages based on the value you deliver - remember, you're not selling time, you're selling outcomes.

### ACTION ITEMS

- ☐ Define your core service packages
- ☐ Create package descriptions
- ☐ Set pricing structure
- ☐ List deliverables for each package
- ☐ Create service timelines
- ☐ Define scope limitations
- ☐ Design upsell paths

### Real-World Examples

Let's explore how AI consultation works in practice by looking at common business scenarios where AI can make a meaningful difference. These aren't hypothetical situations - they're the kinds of opportunities you'll find in almost any business.

Consider a small business drowning in administrative tasks. The opportunity isn't to completely automate their operations - it's to identify specific, time-consuming processes that AI can streamline. Email management, appointment scheduling, and basic customer inquiries are perfect starting points. The key is showing how simple AI implementations can free up hours every week for more valuable work.

Marketing teams face different challenges. They need to create consistent content across multiple channels while maintaining brand voice. AI consultation here focuses on building systematic approaches to content creation and distribution. This might mean developing prompt libraries for different content types, setting up quality control workflows, or creating templates that ensure brand consistency.

Customer service presents clear opportunities for AI enhancement. The goal isn't replacing human support - it's making it more efficient. This could mean implementing AI for initial customer contact, categorizing support tickets, or providing agents with AI-assisted response suggestions. Success comes from showing how AI can support and enhance human customer service rather than replace it.

Workflow optimization shows how AI can improve existing processes rather than replace them. Look for repetitive tasks that slow down operations: document processing, data entry, basic analysis, or report generation. The opportunity is to build systems that handle routine work while flagging exceptions for human review.

The key to successful implementation isn't pushing the latest AI technology - it's identifying specific business problems where AI can deliver measurable improvements. Focus on solutions that can be implemented quickly, show clear results, and deliver obvious value. This practical approach helps businesses see AI as a tool for improvement rather than a mysterious technology.

> **ACTION ITEMS**
>
> - ☐ Document 3 case study templates
> - ☐ Create implementation roadmaps
> - ☐ List common solution patterns
> - ☐ Build ROI calculation templates
> - ☐ Prepare client success stories
> - ☐ Create before/after scenarios
> - ☐ Document common pitfalls

### Delivery Process

A systematic delivery process transforms your AI knowledge into consistent, professional results for clients. This isn't about following rigid procedures - it's about having reliable frameworks that ensure you deliver value every time.

Start with a structured initial consultation that goes beyond surface discussions. Your framework should help clients articulate their real challenges, not just their perceived AI needs. Ask about their current processes, pain points, and what success looks like for them. This initial conversation sets expectations and helps you understand where AI can make the biggest impact.

Your assessment methodology keeps you focused on finding practical opportunities. Examine workflows, review existing tools, and identify bottlenecks. Look for patterns: repetitive tasks that consume time, processes that scale poorly, or areas where consistency is challenging. Document everything systematically - these observations become the foundation for your recommendations.

Developing recommendations is where your expertise really shines. Transform your assessment findings into clear, actionable plans. Break down implementations into phases, starting with quick wins that build confidence. Be specific about tools, costs, and expected outcomes. Most importantly, explain your recommendations in business terms, not technical jargon.

Implementation support requires clear processes. Create checklists for tool setup, documentation templates for procedures, and frameworks for testing. Build in regular checkpoints to ensure everything's working as intended. Your role is to guide the implementation while helping clients develop their internal capabilities.

Progress tracking keeps everything on course. Establish clear metrics tied to business outcomes - time saved, tasks automated, quality improved. Regular check-ins help identify and resolve issues early. Document successes and challenges; this information improves your processes and builds your knowledge base.

Client communication ties everything together. Regular updates, clear documentation, and prompt responses build confidence. Create templates for common communications, but personalize them for each client's situation. Your communication should make clients feel supported while keeping projects moving forward.

### ACTION ITEMS

- ☐ Create client onboarding process
- ☐ Build assessment frameworks
- ☐ Set up progress tracking system
- ☐ Create communication templates
- ☐ Define success metrics
- ☐ Build reporting templates
- ☐ Document quality controls

### Growth & Scaling

Growing an AI consultation practice isn't about working with more clients - it's about delivering more value systematically. Each successful project becomes a foundation for attracting better opportunities and developing more valuable services.

Your reputation grows through documented results. Every successful implementation becomes a story worth telling. Document the challenges you solve, the systems you build, and the improvements you deliver. Focus on specific outcomes: processes streamlined, time saved, or operations improved. These aren't just case studies - they're proof of your ability to deliver real business value.

Referral systems grow naturally when you deliver consistent value. Make it easy for satisfied clients to share their experiences. Create simple ways for them to introduce you to other businesses facing similar challenges. Your best marketing comes from clients explaining how you helped them implement AI effectively.

Partnership opportunities emerge as you work with different businesses. Build relationships with complementary service providers - business consultants, software developers, or efficiency experts who see where AI could help their clients. These partnerships work best when they're based on mutual value rather than formal agreements.

Service expansion follows natural paths. As you work with clients, you'll spot patterns in their needs. Maybe your implementation clients need ongoing support. Perhaps your assessment clients want help with team training. Let your services grow based on real demand rather than assumptions about what might work.

The key to scaling isn't doing more - it's leveraging your expertise more effectively. Build systems that let you deliver consistent value efficiently. Focus on opportunities that match your strengths and deliver clear value to clients.

## ACTION ITEMS

- ☐ Create case study documentation system
- ☐ Build referral tracking process
- ☐ Identify potential strategic partners
- ☐ Set growth metrics and KPIs
- ☐ Create scaling procedures
- ☐ Document successful client stories
- ☐ Plan service expansion roadmap
- ☐ Build resource scaling plan
- ☐ Create client feedback system
- ☐ Set up partnership agreements

**Chapter Summary**

You've just learned how to build an AI consultation practice that delivers real value to businesses. The key isn't becoming an AI expert - it's building systematic approaches to helping businesses implement AI effectively. Your experience with AI tools, combined with your business understanding, positions you perfectly to guide companies through practical AI implementation.

Start small but think systematically. Begin with AI readiness assessments for a single client type, documenting your process and results carefully. Build your frameworks and templates as you go. Each project teaches you something new about what businesses need and how to deliver it effectively.

Your next steps are straightforward: identify a specific type of business you want to help, develop your assessment framework, and create your first service package. Focus on delivering measurable value and documenting your results. Remember, you're not selling AI expertise - you're selling business improvement through practical AI implementation.

In the next chapter, we'll explore Advanced AI Strategies, where you'll learn how to expand your services with more sophisticated AI implementations. The consultation foundation you've built here will help you deliver even more value as you grow your capabilities.

For now, focus on building your first consultation framework. The businesses struggling with AI implementation need your systematic approach more than they realize. Your opportunity is helping them bridge the gap between AI possibilities and practical business results.

## KEY TAKEAWAYS

- Focus on solving specific business problems rather than selling AI technology
- Position yourself as a practical implementation guide rather than a technical expert
- Start with business challenges, then identify where AI can make a meaningful difference
- Build systematic assessment frameworks to evaluate AI opportunities consistently
- Create solution blueprints for common implementations to avoid reinventing the wheel
- Package services clearly: Assessment, Implementation Planning, Tool Setup, Training, Advisory
- Document everything - processes, results, and improvements
- Focus on quick wins that build client confidence in AI implementation
- Create clear metrics tied to business outcomes, not technical capabilities
- Target businesses large enough to invest but too small for full-time AI staff
- Build a library of case studies showing concrete business results
- Develop clear, practical documentation that clients can actually use
- Grow through referrals and partnerships with complementary service providers
- Price based on business value delivered rather than time spent
- Start with a specific client type rather than trying to serve everyone

CHAPTER 10

# Advanced AI Strategies

## Opening Hook

Throughout this book, we've explored various AI side hustles that you can start quickly and run alongside your day job. But there's another level of opportunity emerging: the chance to build AI-powered products and platforms that could grow into something much bigger.

The timing is perfect for ambitious AI projects. The tools have matured enough to be reliable, but the market is still young enough that there's room for innovative solutions. You don't need to be a machine learning expert or have a team of developers. Modern AI platforms and development tools make it possible to build sophisticated applications with relatively modest technical resources.

Think about education platforms that adapt to each student's learning style, business tools that automate complex workflows, or consumer apps that make AI capabilities accessible to everyone. These aren't just theoretical possibilities - they're opportunities you can start exploring while maintaining your current income.

The key is starting small but thinking big. Begin with a focused solution to a specific problem, but build it in a way that can scale. Use your evenings and weekends to validate ideas, create prototypes, and test with real users. Many successful AI companies started as side projects before growing into full-fledged businesses.

In this chapter, we'll explore how to go beyond service businesses and build AI-powered products that could become something bigger. You'll learn practical approaches to product development, technical considerations for building AI applications, and strategies for growing while managing risk. Whether you want to create the next big AI platform or just build something more scalable than services, this is your roadmap to bigger opportunities.

## AI Product Development

Building AI-powered products isn't about cramming artificial intelligence into every feature - it's about using AI strategically to solve real problems better than traditional solutions. The most successful AI products often start with a simple premise: take something people already need, and make it significantly better through AI.

Education platforms represent a particularly exciting opportunity. Imagine a language learning app that adapts not just to skill level, but to learning style and interests. Or a math tutor that identifies exactly where a student is struggling and adjusts its teaching approach accordingly. The key is focusing on specific learning challenges that AI is uniquely suited to solve, rather than trying to reinvent education entirely.

Business tools offer another rich territory for AI products. Look for repetitive tasks that plague specific industries. A contract analysis tool for small law firms, an inventory prediction system for retail shops, or a customer insight platform for local businesses. Success comes from solving focused problems extremely well, not trying to be everything for everyone.

Consumer apps need to make AI accessible without making it obvious. Think about apps that enhance photos based on artistic principles, writing assistants that help people sound more professional, or personal finance advisors that offer Netflix-style recommendations for money management. The best consumer AI products feel magical but familiar.

Market validation becomes critical before diving too deep. Start by building a simple landing page describing your product idea. Use paid ads or social media to drive traffic and gauge interest. Talk to potential users about their problems, not your solution. You'll often find that your initial idea needs adjustment based on real feedback.

Your MVP (Minimum Viable Product) should focus on one core AI-powered feature that delivers clear value. Don't try to match every feature of existing products plus AI. Instead, do one thing so well that users will overlook missing secondary features. This might mean starting with a browser extension instead of a full app, or a Telegram bot instead of a complete platform.

Remember, you're not just building a product - you're creating a solution that could grow into something bigger. Keep your initial scope manageable, but architect your solution in a way that can scale when success comes.

### ACTION ITEMS

- ☐ Write down 3 specific problems your product will solve
- ☐ Create a simple landing page on Carrd.co or similar
- ☐ Set up Google Analytics and a $50 test ad campaign
- ☐ Build one working feature (ignore everything else)
- ☐ Test with 5 real potential users
- ☐ Record exact time/cost to serve each user
- ☐ List 3 specific ways the product could break
- ☐ Calculate basic cost per user

#### Custom Model Development

While existing AI models can handle many tasks effectively, there are times when a custom-trained or fine-tuned model makes sense. The key is recognizing when the investment in custom development will deliver enough value to justify the additional complexity and cost.

Consider custom model development when you have specific needs that general models can't quite meet. Maybe you need a model that understands your industry's specialized terminology, or one that can recognize patterns unique to your target market. The best candidates for custom development are narrow, well-defined problems where you have access to quality training data.

Fine-tuning existing models offers a middle ground between using off-the-shelf solutions and building from scratch. Starting with a pre-trained model and adjusting it for your specific use case can deliver impressive results with relatively modest investment. This might mean fine-tuning a language model on your industry's documentation, or adapting an image model to recognize specific types of products.

Data preparation becomes crucial for success. You'll need clean, well-organized datasets that represent the problems you're trying to solve. Start collecting and organizing relevant data early - this often takes longer than expected. Focus on quality over quantity; a smaller dataset of high-quality, well-labeled examples often outperforms larger but messier data.

Training considerations extend beyond just technical setup. You'll need to think about computing resources, training time, and iteration cycles. Cloud platforms offer scalable solutions, but costs can add up quickly. Start with smaller experiments to validate your approach before committing to full-scale training. Monitor your metrics carefully to avoid overfitting or wasting resources on unproductive training runs.

Deployment brings its own challenges. Consider where your model will run - in the cloud, on local servers, or on user devices. Each option has tradeoffs in terms of cost, latency, and user experience. Build your deployment pipeline with monitoring and updates in mind. You'll need ways to track performance, gather feedback, and roll out improvements over time.

### ACTION ITEMS

- ☐ Collect 100 specific examples of your use case
- ☐ Clean and label 20 test examples
- ☐ Set up a free/basic Colab account
- ☐ Choose between fine-tuning or training from scratch
- ☐ Calculate exact GPU hours needed
- ☐ Test model with 10 real-world examples
- ☐ Measure response time and costs
- ☐ Document every prompt that works

## Advanced Automation Systems

Advanced automation isn't just about connecting more tools - it's about building resilient systems that can handle complex tasks reliably at scale. Think of it as creating a digital assembly line where multiple AI models work together seamlessly, each handling the part of the task it does best.

Multi-model orchestration becomes crucial as your systems grow more sophisticated. You might use one model for initial text analysis, another for content generation, and a third for quality checking. The key is managing these interactions smoothly. Build systems that can route tasks to the right model, handle the handoffs between models, and maintain context throughout the process.

Complex workflows need sophisticated automation. Instead of simple if-then sequences, create adaptive systems that can handle variations and edge cases. Your automation should be able to recognize different types of inputs, route them appropriately, and adjust processing based on context. Build in decision points where the system can choose different paths based on intermediate results.

Quality assurance becomes critical at scale. Implement automated checks at key points in your workflow. Use validation models to verify outputs, compare results against expected patterns, and flag potential issues for review. The goal isn't to eliminate human oversight entirely, but to ensure that human attention focuses on cases that truly need it.

Error handling and recovery separate professional systems from amateur attempts. Your automation needs to gracefully handle API outages, model failures, or unexpected inputs. Build retry mechanisms with exponential backoff, implement fallback options for critical functions, and ensure your system can recover cleanly from interruptions. Most importantly, make sure errors are logged clearly for later analysis.

Performance optimization requires systematic monitoring and improvement. Track key metrics like processing time, success rates, and resource usage. Look for bottlenecks where tasks queue up or resources get constrained. Build dashboards that give you clear visibility into system health and performance trends. Use this data to guide improvements and capacity planning.

Remember, advanced automation is about building systems that scale with your success. Start with solid foundations in error handling and monitoring, then grow your automation's complexity as your needs evolve.

### ACTION ITEMS

- ☐ List every API and tool you'll connect
- ☐ Write down exact costs per API call
- ☐ Create error message templates
- ☐ Set up basic Slack/email alerts
- ☐ Test each connection individually
- ☐ Document retry limits for each step
- ☐ Create a "kill switch" procedure
- ☐ Set up basic cost tracking

## Building AI-Powered Apps

Creating AI-powered applications requires thinking differently about software architecture. You're not just building a traditional app with some AI features bolted on - you're designing systems where AI capabilities are central to the user experience. This changes how you approach everything from data flow to user interface design.

Start with architecture that supports AI integration. Your app needs to handle asynchronous processing smoothly, manage model interactions efficiently, and scale with demand. Consider using microservices architecture to separate AI processing from other app functions. This lets you update AI components without disrupting the entire application and makes it easier to handle the unique resource requirements of AI processing.

Technology stack selection becomes crucial for success. Modern frameworks like Next.js, Flask, or FastAPI make it easier to build AI-powered web applications. Choose tools that support both rapid development and future scaling. Your backend needs to handle AI model interactions efficiently, while your frontend should manage loading states and results gracefully. Consider serverless platforms for easier scaling and cost management.

AI integration patterns need careful thought. Will your models run in real-time or process requests asynchronously? How will you handle model updates? Build patterns for caching results, managing API quotas, and handling model failures. Consider implementing a queue system for longer-running AI tasks, with status updates to keep users informed of progress.

User experience design for AI applications brings unique challenges. Users need to understand what the AI can and can't do, without getting lost in technical details. Design clear feedback mechanisms so users know when AI is processing their request. Build intuitive ways to refine or adjust AI outputs. Most importantly, design interfaces that make AI feel like a natural part of the workflow, not a bolted-on feature.

Testing requires a comprehensive approach. Beyond traditional unit and integration tests, you need strategies for testing AI interactions. Build test suites that verify model inputs and outputs, check error handling, and validate the entire user experience. Include performance testing to ensure your app remains responsive even under AI processing load. Consider implementing A/B testing to optimize AI interactions.

Deployment needs careful planning. Consider using containerization for consistent environments across development and production. Set up monitoring for both application metrics and AI performance. Plan for model updates and versioning. Build deployment pipelines that can handle the unique requirements of AI components, including model file distribution and version management.

### ACTION ITEMS

- [ ] Choose between Next.js or Flask (pick one)
- [ ] Set up free tier on Vercel/Railway
- [ ] Create API rate limiting rules
- [ ] Build loading states for AI features
- [ ] Set up error logging with Sentry
- [ ] Test with slow internet
- [ ] Measure response times
- [ ] Calculate costs per user action

**Premium Service Opportunities**

As you build expertise in advanced AI implementation, opportunities emerge for premium services that go beyond basic consulting. These high-value offerings combine your technical knowledge with business acumen to solve complex challenges for clients willing to pay for expertise.

High-value consulting becomes possible when you can guide organizations through sophisticated AI implementations. This isn't about simple tool recommendations - it's about architecting complete solutions that transform business operations. Focus on engagements where you can demonstrate clear ROI through cost savings, efficiency gains, or revenue improvements. Your value comes from understanding both the technical possibilities and business implications.

Custom development services represent another premium opportunity. Organizations often need specialized AI solutions that don't exist off-the-shelf. This might mean building custom models for specific industries, developing proprietary automation systems, or creating unique AI-powered applications. Position these services based on the business value they deliver, not just the technical work involved.

Training programs offer a way to scale your expertise. Develop workshops and courses that help organizations build internal AI capabilities. Focus on practical skills that teams can apply immediately. Consider offering different levels - from basic AI literacy for general staff to advanced implementation techniques for technical teams. Package these as both public workshops and custom corporate training.

Enterprise solutions require a different approach than small business services. Large organizations need comprehensive solutions that integrate with existing systems, scale across departments, and meet strict security requirements. While these projects take longer to land and require more resources to deliver, they also command premium pricing and often lead to long-term relationships.

Pricing these premium services requires confidence in your value proposition. Move away from hourly rates toward value-based pricing that reflects the business impact of your solutions. Consider tiered pricing models that offer different levels of support and involvement. Don't be afraid to price significantly higher than basic services - organizations expect to pay more for premium expertise and comprehensive solutions.

> **ACTION ITEMS**
>
> ☐ Create 3 specific service tiers
> ☐ List exact deliverables for each tier
> ☐ Calculate your hourly minimum rate
> ☐ Write 3 sample proposals
> ☐ Create a client questionnaire
> ☐ Build a basic service contract
> ☐ Set up project milestone templates
> ☐ Create a "red flags" list

## Future-Proofing Strategies

Success in AI isn't just about what you build today - it's about staying relevant as the technology evolves. The field moves quickly, but that creates opportunities for those who can adapt and grow strategically.

Staying current with AI developments doesn't mean chasing every new model or feature. Instead, focus on understanding fundamental shifts in capabilities and their practical implications. Follow key AI platforms and their development roadmaps. Pay attention to how leading companies are implementing AI successfully. Most importantly, regularly experiment with new tools and approaches in low-risk ways.

Adapting to model changes becomes easier when you build your systems with change in mind. Design your applications and workflows to be model-agnostic where possible. Keep your AI integrations modular so you can swap out components as better options emerge. Document your requirements clearly so you can evaluate new models against your actual needs rather than just their marketing promises.

Maintaining competitive advantage comes from focusing on value delivery rather than specific technologies. Your real advantage isn't in the AI tools you use - it's in how you apply them to solve real problems. Keep deepening your understanding of your clients' industries and challenges. Build systems and processes that can evolve with technology while consistently delivering results.

Risk management becomes increasingly important as your AI implementations grow more sophisticated. Diversify your technology dependencies so you're not overly reliant on any single platform or model. Keep security and privacy considerations central to your planning. Build redundancy into critical systems and maintain clear backup plans for potential failures.

Growth planning needs to balance ambition with practicality. Look for opportunities to scale what's working while maintaining quality. Consider strategic partnerships that could accelerate your growth. Keep building your knowledge base and documentation so you can train others as you expand. Most importantly, stay focused on delivering real value - that's what creates sustainable growth in a rapidly changing field.

### ACTION ITEMS

- ☐ Subscribe to 2-3 specific AI newsletters
- ☐ Set monthly budget for testing new tools
- ☐ List backup options for each core tool
- ☐ Calculate emergency fund needed
- ☐ Document current tech stack costs
- ☐ Set quarterly review dates
- ☐ Create basic disaster recovery plan
- ☐ List alternative tools for each service

### Chapter Summary

You've just explored how to take your AI side hustle beyond basic services into more ambitious territory. The key isn't trying to build the next ChatGPT - it's finding specific problems where AI can create unique value, then building solutions that can grow with your success.

Start small but architect for growth. Begin with a focused AI product that solves a specific problem well, or develop premium services that leverage your growing expertise. Build your systems with scalability in mind, but don't let complexity slow down your initial launch. Each project teaches you something valuable about building AI-powered solutions that last.

Your next steps are straightforward: identify a specific opportunity where AI could create significant value, develop a minimal but scalable solution, and test it with real users. Focus on building something that could grow bigger while still managing it alongside your current commitments. Remember, you're not just building features - you're creating solutions that could evolve into something much larger.

In the next chapter, we'll explore how to manage your growing AI side hustle effectively, including time management, legal considerations, and balancing it with your full-time work. The advanced capabilities you've learned here will need solid business foundations to thrive.

For now, focus on identifying your first advanced AI opportunity. Whether it's building a product, developing premium services, or creating sophisticated automation systems, the market needs solutions from people who understand both AI's capabilities and real-world business needs.

# THE AI SIDE HUSTLE REVOLUTION

## KEY TAKEAWAYS

- Start small but architect for scalability from the beginning
- Focus on solving specific problems better through AI rather than adding AI to everything
- Validate market interest before diving deep into development
- Build MVPs around one core AI-powered feature that delivers clear value
- Consider custom model development only when justified by specific needs
- Design automation systems that can handle complexity and scale reliably
- Implement thorough error handling and monitoring from the start
- Build AI-powered apps with architecture that supports AI integration at its core
- Create premium service offerings based on advanced AI implementation expertise
- Price based on business value delivered rather than technical complexity
- Stay current with AI developments while focusing on fundamental capabilities
- Design systems to be model-agnostic where possible
- Maintain competitive advantage through problem-solving rather than specific technologies
- Balance growth ambition with practical risk management
- Document everything to support future scaling and training

CHAPTER 11

# Your AI Journey: Next Steps

Congratulations! You've learned the foundations of building an AI-powered side hustle. From basic service arbitrage to advanced AI products, you now understand the landscape of opportunities and have practical frameworks for getting started. But this isn't the end of your journey - it's just the beginning.

Success in AI entrepreneurship requires continuous learning and adaptation. While this book has focused on AI-specific business models and implementation strategies, there are several adjacent skills and resources you'll want to explore as your business grows.

## Essential Skills to Develop

Your AI expertise is just one piece of the puzzle. As your business grows, you'll want to develop complementary skills that make your AI implementations more effective. Start with business fundamentals - understanding basic accounting, legal structures, and tax implications will help you make better decisions. You don't need to become an expert in these areas, but knowing when and how to seek professional help is crucial.

Technical skills become increasingly valuable as you tackle more sophisticated projects. Consider learning basic programming concepts, database management, or web development. Again, you don't need to become a full-stack developer, but understanding these areas helps you better architect AI solutions and communicate with technical partners.

Marketing and sales capabilities often determine the difference between a good idea and a successful business. Focus on learning how to communicate the value of your AI solutions effectively. Understanding digital marketing, content creation, and sales processes helps you attract and convert the right clients.

---

**ACTION ITEMS**

- ☐ Sign up for a basic accounting course (Udemy/Coursera)
- ☐ Create a business checking account
- ☐ Set up a simple bookkeeping system (Wave/QuickBooks)
- ☐ Learn one programming language (Python recommended)
- ☐ Build a basic portfolio website
- ☐ Write 3 case studies of your work
- ☐ Create templates for client proposals
- ☐ Set up a CRM (free tier of HubSpot/similar)

---

## Building Your Support System

No successful entrepreneur operates in isolation. Start building your support network early. Find mentors who have experience in AI businesses or similar technical ventures. They can help you avoid common pitfalls and see opportunities you might miss.

Join AI communities and professional groups. Online forums, Discord servers, and local meetups are great places to share experiences, learn about new developments, and find potential partners. Look for communities that focus on practical implementation rather than just technical discussions.

Stay current with AI developments, but be selective about where you focus your attention. Follow key AI platforms' development blogs, join relevant professional associations, and set up news alerts for your specific area of focus. The goal isn't to chase every new development, but to understand trends that could affect your business.

> **ACTION ITEMS**
>
> ☐ Join 2 AI Discord communities
> ☐ Attend one local tech meetup
> ☐ Find one mentor (reach out to 5 potential mentors)
> ☐ Subscribe to 2 specific AI newsletters
> ☐ Set up Google Alerts for your niche
> ☐ Join relevant LinkedIn groups
> ☐ Create a Twitter list of AI experts
> ☐ Schedule monthly learning time

### Common Challenges and Solutions

Every growing business faces hurdles, but AI businesses have some unique challenges. Resource management becomes crucial as you scale - both computing resources and human expertise. Learn to balance automation with human oversight, and build systems that can grow without breaking.

Know when to seek professional help. As your business grows, you'll likely need legal advice for terms of service and data handling, accounting help for financial planning, and possibly technical expertise for more complex implementations. Build relationships with professionals who understand the unique aspects of AI businesses.

Most importantly, maintain perspective on what matters. It's easy to get caught up in technical details or chase the latest AI developments. Remember that your success comes from solving real problems for real clients. Keep your focus on delivering value, and let that guide your growth decisions.

> **ACTION ITEMS**
>
> - ☐ Calculate monthly tool/API costs
> - ☐ Set up cost monitoring alerts
> - ☐ Create an emergency contact list
> - ☐ Find a tech-savvy lawyer
> - ☐ Set up an AI tools backup plan
> - ☐ Document common problem solutions
> - ☐ Create client onboarding checklist
> - ☐ Set up basic error monitoring

## Final Thoughts

You're starting your AI journey at an incredible time. The technology is mature enough to be reliable but still new enough that there's room for innovation. Your opportunity isn't just to use AI tools - it's to create solutions that make AI's capabilities accessible and valuable to others.

Start small but think strategically. Begin with the models and approaches we've discussed, but always build with growth in mind. Learn from each project, document your successes and failures, and keep refining your approach. Remember, every successful AI business started with a single implementation.

The road ahead will have challenges, but you now have the frameworks and knowledge to tackle them effectively. Focus on delivering real value, build systems that can scale, and never stop learning. The AI revolution is just beginning, and you're well-positioned to be part of it.

Your next step is simple: choose one of the business models we've discussed and start implementing it. Don't wait for perfect conditions or complete knowledge. Start small, learn from real experience, and grow systematically. The best time to begin your AI journey is now.

### KEY TAKEAWAYS

- Balance AI expertise with essential business skills like accounting, legal, and marketing
- Develop basic technical literacy to better architect and implement AI solutions
- Build a strong support network including mentors and professional communities
- Focus on practical implementation rather than chasing every new AI development
- Know when to seek professional help for legal, financial, and technical matters
- Stay current with AI trends but be selective about where you focus your attention
- Document both successes and failures to refine your approach over time
- Start small but build with scalability in mind from the beginning
- Prioritize solving real problems over technical sophistication
- Build systems that balance automation with appropriate human oversight
- Maintain focus on delivering value rather than chasing the latest AI developments
- Develop effective ways to communicate the value of your AI solutions
- Join relevant communities and professional groups for ongoing learning
- Create a sustainable approach to resource management as you scale
- Begin implementation now rather than waiting for perfect conditions

www.ingramcontent.com/pod-product-compliance
Lightning Source LLC
Chambersburg PA
CBHW071052240526
45471CB00015B/1707